Hiking Waterfalls in Oregon

Oregon

A Guide to the State's
Best Waterfall Hikes

Adam Sawyer

FALCONGUIDES

GUILFORD, CONNECTICUT
HELENA, MONTANA
AN IMPRINT OF ROWMAN & LITTLEFIELD

The author and Rowman & Littlefield assume no liability for accidents happening to, or injuries sustained by, readers who engage in the activities described in this book.

Contents

The Hikes

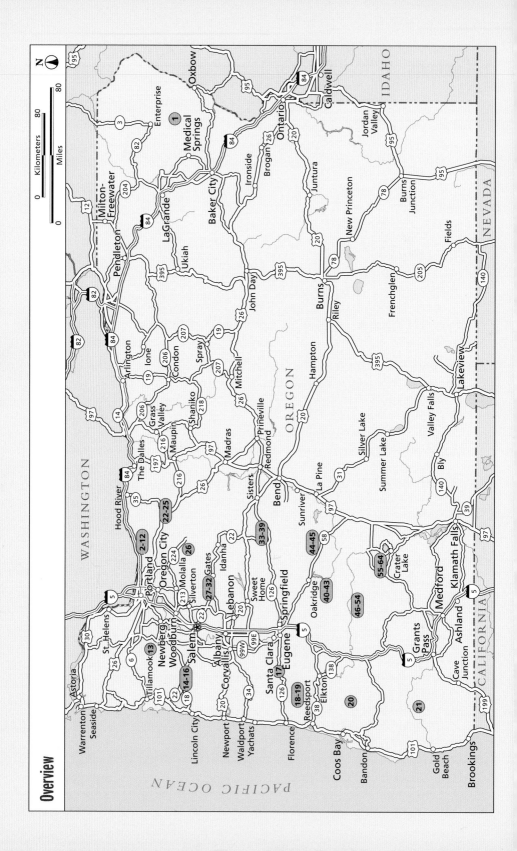

Overview

Southern Oregon Cascades 163

Acknowledgments

This book would not have been possible without the support and aid of a great number of people. For starters, my ex-wife, Krystin Sawyer, who supported my decision to leave the security of the corporate world, downsize our lives, and let me try to make a living hiking. I can't thank you enough for your support and faith in me.

I would also like to thank everyone that ever drove my car-less self to a hike: Heather Egizio, Laurilyn Hepler, Matt Hazelrig, Mac Barrett, Dottie Barrett, Clary Barrett, and Danny Chase.

Extra special thanks go to the ladies that drove me or provided the means for me to drive to the farthest reaches of Oregon. Kassidy Anderson, thank you for taking us all over central and eastern Oregon and for hiking with me even when illness brought you to tears. Stephanie Paris, thank you for providing the BMW, funding, and navigational skill that delivered us to sixty-three waterfalls over the course of seventeen glorious days last summer. You endured gravel roads, mosquito bites, logging trucks, bears, and swarming ants with almost superhuman aplomb. I am eternally grateful.

Big thanks also go to all of the people who provided logistical support along the way in the name of helping others discover Oregon: Katherine Hoppe, Kristine McConnell, Sue Price, Molly Blancett, Brad Rasmussen, and Greg Lief. Thanks to Bryan Swan and his Northwest Waterfall Survey. Most of the heights for the waterfalls listed in this book were retrieved from his website, waterfallsnorthwest.com.

Thanks to portlandhikers.org, William Sullivan, Scott Cook, Paul Gerald, Tom Kloster, Marcy Cottrell Houle, Doug Lorain, Laura Foster, Bart Blasengame, and Oregon Field Guide, who all provided inspiration, guidance, support, or all of the above.

Thanks to Columbia Sportswear for the gear I used to stay warm and dry. Thanks to Garmin for the GPS that documented the whole thing. And big thanks to KEEN footwear. It is an honor to serve as an ambassador for a company that does things the right way. I was privileged to have a pair of KEENs on for literally every step of this journey.

Thanks to the friends and family who provided unending support: Jade Sawyer Chase, Janaira Quigley, William Sawyer, Cindy Sawyer, Scott Stearns, Jonathan McCabe, Holly Vanderpool, Morgan Hecht, Anna Haller, Rebekah Voie, Dan Wakefield, Abigail Entrican, Marc Alan Jordan, Carlye Hechtman, the Portland community of St. Johns, Portland Walking Tours, countless others not named here, and every nature-loving person I've ever shared words or beers with.

Sincerest of thanks go to Lucy Gibson and Allen Cox. None if this would have been possible without your belief in the new guy. That is a fact.

Finally, this book is dedicated to my daughter, Thea. We discovered waterfalls and hiking together. Though at the time you were only 5 years old, your love of the outdoors inspired me even more than my own newfound fascination. Thank you for never allowing me to go on a backpacking trip alone. I hope that you will eventually see every waterfall in this book . . . and that you'll allow me to tag along on a few.

Introduction

I am not from Oregon. As a matter of fact, Portland is roughly the twentieth US city that I've lived in. In my previous career I was an information technology specialist. While living in Florida I accepted a position in Vancouver, Washington. A driving force behind this decision was the fact that I had yet to live in the Northwest. I didn't think I was going to like it, but as a wanderer, I wanted to check the area off my list.

After a few months of work and settling in, my family and I took a drive into the Columbia River Gorge on a warm summer day and my life was changed. I had never seen a waterfall before, and suddenly they were everywhere. Children were swimming in their splash pools, families were getting their photos taken in front of them, and some people were walking along paths that led to the top of them and beyond. I was stunned.

I was never much of a nature person. I didn't grow up hiking. But I was so taken by what I had witnessed on that first trip into the gorge that weekend excursions to waterfalls quickly became the norm. Soon thereafter, weekday trips after work crept into my schedule. Seeking out new waterfalls became an addiction. At the same time, I was growing more and more dissatisfied with my career. Staff reductions in the company I worked for meant an increased workload. I was on-call half of the time, and on-call backup the other half. I slept with a BlackBerry on my pillow and more often than not woke up numerous times throughout the evening to address work issues. But the money was good. And I thought that if I could sock enough of it away, I could retire early and live life.

My obsession with the outdoors was escalating at the same rate that my job satisfaction was plummeting. I had a view of Mount Hood from my office and it was quickly becoming a serious distraction. I was no longer an effective employee and I was no longer willing to sacrifice my physical and mental well-being so that *someday* I could enjoy life, assuming I was still able to do so. So I quit.

With the support of my family, we downsized our lives and I left my career as an IT specialist behind. The initial plan was to make a go at being a professional photographer. What I quickly discovered was that being a landscape photographer in the Northwest is akin to being an actor in Hollywood. Everybody does it. And I also quickly discovered that I was doggy-paddling in the shallow end of the Northwest talent pool of photographers. So I broadened my scope. With the goal of getting paid to be outdoors, I settled into a career as a storyteller. Between writing, photography, and my work as a walking-tour guide, I now pay the bills by telling stories with spoken word, written word, and photographs. The paychecks might be smaller, but I've never been happier.

My work now takes me all over the Northwest. And thanks to this book, over darn near every hill and dale in the state of Oregon. This guidebook is not written from the perspective of someone who was born and raised here—someone who knows the landscape like the back of his hand. This book was written with the exuberance and perspective of a man who saw a waterfall for the first time in his mid-thirties and had his life path permanently and thankfully altered by the experience.

I am not from Oregon. But I am an Oregonian.

What follows is a collection of my favorite waterfall hikes in the state of Oregon. In some cases it's all about the waterfall. In others, the scenery or uniqueness of the hike combined with the waterfalls make the journey a standout. Also included are a number of falls that you can drive up to or that require a very short walk from the parking area. That being stated, there are numerous unofficial trails in the state that lead to what seems like an unending number of waterfalls. Even if you hit every hike in this book, you'll have just scratched the surface of what Oregon holds. I also recommend that you revisit falls in different seasons, under varying weather conditions, and even different times of the day. There is always something new to see.

A Note on Photography

The photographs in this book are not "Photoshopped," enhanced, or manipulated in any way other than contrast, cropping, and, on rare occasion, color correction. My goal is to create photos that capture the essence of the location. As closely as possible, I want the photos to be an exact representation of the look and feel of the scene the way it was in person, in that moment—beautiful but attainable. As a result, I typically don't do long exposure shots unless the low light calls for it. My preference is to leave nature natural.

How to Use This Guide

The waterfall hikes in this book are grouped by geographic area. Each hike is laid out in the same format: a brief introduction, a list of specifics (distance, elevation gain, difficulty, etc.), directions to the trailhead, a description of the hike, a map, and the exact mileage and directions for the hike. I have also included GPS coordinates for the trailheads and waterfalls in each hike.

The elevation gain listed for each hike details the total amount of elevation that will be gained throughout the course of the hike. For example, if a hike starts at 1,000 feet and ascends directly to 1,500 feet, the hike will have an elevation gain of 500 feet. However, if there were undulations in that hike that cause you to ascend and descend, I calculate that into the equation. So in some cases a hike that starts out at 1,000 feet and ends at 1,500 could have 700 feet of elevation gain.

Unless otherwise noted, the mileages listed for each hike assume that you are taking all recommended side routes to viewpoints and the like.

A lot of effort has gone into giving the best driving and hiking directions possible. However, trail conditions change regularly. Trails can be rerouted and access roads closed for any number of reasons. It's a good idea to check weather, road, and trail conditions before any hike.

For Your Safety

It's important to have a very healthy respect for Mother Nature when hiking. Conditions in Oregon are notorious for changing rapidly and with little or no warning. The "expect the best but prepare for the worst" adage is a great thing to keep in mind when you're preparing to go into the wilderness.

Always let somebody know where you're going and when you plan on being back. Know your limitations, and err on the side of caution. If conditions of any sort are making you uncomfortable, that's a good sign to head back or take appropriate action. You can always return at a later date; it's best if you live to hike another day.

Also, be prepared. Whether you are new to hiking or a seasoned veteran, the ten essentials are something that all hikers should have on hand. Here is a list of the updated essential "systems" hikers should have with them any time they go into the wilderness.

1. Navigation: A map and a compass are mandatory. These can be augmented with things like altimeters and GPS units, but always have a map of the area and a compass.

2. Sun protection: Bring sunglasses, sunscreen, and proper clothing, including a hat.

3. Insulation: Will there be a blizzard on the Timberline Trail in July? Probably not. However, you should have whatever it takes to survive the worst conditions that can be reasonably expected. No matter the season, start your outfit with wicking gear: clothing that is not made of cotton and that can wick moisture away from the body. Dress in layers, especially in cooler weather. Pack extra socks. If things are going to be cold or wet, bring additional layers and rain gear. Whatever the conditions are, avoid cotton.

4. Illumination: Flashlights, headlamps, and LEDs all work. It's good to have a backup or spare batteries.

5. First-aid supplies: It's up to you whether or not to bring such things as allergy pills or latex gloves. At the very least you will need some gauze, bandages, tape, and pain meds. There are many prepackaged kits available that include everything from bare-bones basics to an outdoor aid station.

6. Fire: This includes waterproof matches, disposable lighters, and chemical heat tabs.

7. Repair kit and tools: A knife or multitool is fairly standard. Depending on what you're doing, duct tape and rope can be handy as well.

8. Nutrition: At least enough food for an extra day and night in the wilderness. Nutrition bars, jerky, nuts, and the like all work.

9. Hydration: Always have at least a water bottle or water bladder/reservoir system. You should also have some sort of water treatment or filtration on hand.

10. Emergency shelter: If you're backpacking, the tent you're carrying covers this one. If you're taking a day hike, consider a space blanket, rain gear, or even a trash bag.

Hiking Courtesy

Hiking has its own set of written and unwritten laws that are good to know and adhere to. These courtesies help to ensure a pleasant experience for everyone. Here's a brief list:

- Pack it in, pack it out. Do your best to leave no trace. This goes beyond littering: Little things like nutshells or discarded orange peels should go out with you as well.
- Share the trail. Walk single file. On wider paths you can occasionally stroll side by side, but never take up more than half of the trail. Always yield to the hiker heading uphill. Pass slower hikers on the left, and give them a verbal greeting. It's not nice to sneak up on people.
- Stay on the trail. Always stay on the established trail and never cut switchbacks.
- Hike quietly. Keep noise to a minimum and conversations at a reasonable volume unless you're hiking in bear country. Then announce your presence often.
- Take only pictures. Don't pick flowers, collect rocks, or otherwise disturb flora and fauna. The generations after us are going to want to see the wildflower meadows as well.
- Check trailhead guidelines. Trails occasionally have very specific rules. It's a good idea to give trailhead signage a once-over. In addition to guidelines, there are often important announcements about things like trail conditions.
- Follow guidelines for pets. Most trails allow dogs, but some do not. Check before bringing your pets. Also follow leash laws. There are some trails that don't require dogs to be on leash, but most do. And always clean up after your pet and pack it out.
- Finally, be nice. You don't have to have a full-on conversation with everyone you pass, but a cordial greeting doesn't hurt anything. We're living in a society.

Trail Finder

Author's Favorite Waterfall Hikes

1. Adam Creek Falls
2. Latourell Falls
5. Multnomah/Wahkeena Falls Loop
6. Oneonta Gorge
16. Drift Creek Falls
18. Sweet Creek Falls
20. Golden and Silver Falls
22. Ramona Falls
27. Abiqua Falls
29. Trail of Ten Falls (Silver Falls State Park)
32. Opal Creek
36. Sahalie/Koosah Falls
39. Tumalo Falls
43. Trestle Creek Falls
45. Salt Creek Falls
50. Wolf Creek Falls
52. Yakso Falls

Best Hikes for Backcountry Camping

1. Adam Creek Falls
10. Eagle Creek
32. Opal Creek

Best Swimming Holes

6. Oneonta Gorge
32. Opal Creek
47. Susan Creek Falls
48. Fall Creek Falls
J. Three Pools

Most Crowded Waterfall Hikes

4. Angel's Rest (Coopey Falls)
5. Multnomah/Wahkeena Falls Loop
10. Eagle Creek
29. Trail of Ten Falls (Silver Falls State Park)
39. Tumalo Falls
56. Toketee Falls

Least Crowded Waterfall Hikes

19. Kentucky Falls/North Fork Falls
40. Spirit Falls
41. Moon Falls
42. Pinard Falls
49. Shadow Falls
53. Clover Falls
58. Warm Springs Falls
60. Rough Rider Falls
63. Pearsoney Falls

Best Waterfall Hikes for Kids

3. Bridal Veil Falls
9. Wahclella Falls
16. Drift Creek Falls (if they aren't afraid of bridges)
18. Sweet Creek Falls
25. Little Zigzag Falls
28. Butte Creek Falls
33. McDowell Creek Falls
47. Susan Creek Falls
50. Wolf Creek Falls
59. Lemolo Falls

Most Unique Falls

6. Oneonta Gorge
15. Harts Cove/Chitwood Creek Falls
18. Sweet Creek Falls
26. Pup Creek Falls
32. Opal Creek
37. Proxy Falls
45. Salt Creek Falls
49. Shadow Falls
55. Columnar/Surprise Falls
A. White River Falls

Best Waterfall Hikes for History Buffs

12. Starvation Creek Falls
20. Golden and Silver Falls
32. Opal Creek
35. House Rock Falls
C. Mist Falls

Map Legend

Municipal

≡⟨20⟩≡	Interstate Highway
≡⟨178⟩≡	US Highway
≡⟨107⟩≡	State Road
≡⟨263⟩≡	Local/County Road
≡⟨FR 356⟩≡	Forest Road
= = = =	Unpaved Road
⊢—⊢—⊢	Railroad
— ·· — ·· —	State Boundary

Trails

▪▪▪▪▪▪	Featured Trail
------	Trail
———	Paved Trail

Water Features

◯	Body of Water
≈	Marsh
～	River/Creek
⌢⌒	Intermittent Stream
≋	Waterfall
⌀⁻	Spring

Land Management

🔺	National Park/Forest
🔺	National Monument/Wilderness Area
🔺	State/County Park

Symbols

▬	Bench
≍	Bridge
▲	Backcountry Campground
▥	Boardwalk/Steps
➤	Boat Launch
■	Building/Point of Interest
⋀	Campground
⌇⌇	Cliff
⌶	Gate
ⵜ	Lighthouse
🅿	Parking
⌣⌢	Pass
▲	Peak/Elevation
🐿	Picnic Area
⛺	Ranger Station/Park Office
🚻	Restroom
🖼	Scenic View
⾕	Tower
○	Town
⟨20⟩	Trailhead
❓	Visitor/Information Center

xiv

Columbia Plateau

Camping and Accommodations

Imperial River Lodge: On the banks of the Deschutes River, the lodge features an outdoor fire pit, restaurant, horseshoes, volleyball court, and riverside porch swings. 304 Bakeoven Rd., Maupin, OR 97037; (800) 395-3903; deschutesriver.com

Wallowa Lake Lodge: Historic lodge on the south end of Wallowa Lake. Built in the 1920s, the lodge features a restaurant and private cabins. 60060 Wallowa Lake Hwy., Joseph, OR 97846; (541) 432-9821; wallowalake.com

Wallowa Lake State Park: 215 total sites, $5 to $38 a night. 72214 Marina Ln., Joseph, OR 97846; (541) 432-4185

Shady Campground: Seven sites, $5 a night. (541) 523-6391

Two Pan Campground: Five sites, $5 a night. (541) 523-6391

1 Adam Creek Falls

The trek to Ice Lake is the premier waterfall hike in eastern Oregon. The numerous named and unnamed cascades that tumble along Adam Creek are certainly a big draw. But it's the scenery of the Wallowa Mountains that makes this classic 15.4-mile out-and-back day hike or overnight backpacking trip get better with every mile. If you're not up for the big trip, the much more attainable BC Falls can be reached from the same trailhead.

Height: Ice Falls, 480 feet; Beauty Falls, 70 feet; BC Falls, 50 feet
Distance: 15.4 miles out and back to Ice Lake, 2.6 miles out and back to BC Falls
Elevation gain: Ice Falls, 3,200 feet; BC Falls, 700 feet
Difficulty: Difficult to Ice Falls, easy to BC Falls
Trail surface: Hard-packed dirt, rocky, occasional talus
Hiking time: About 5–10 total hours

County: Wallowa
Land status: Wilderness
Fees and permits: None
Trail contact: Eagle Cap Ranger District, 201 E. 2nd St., Joseph, OR 97846; (541) 426-5509; www.fs.fed.us/or http://fs.usda.gov/wallowa-whitman
Map: *DeLorme Atlas & Gazetteer Oregon,* page 75, E10

Finding the trailhead: From La Grande, follow OR 82 for 78 miles to Wallowa Lake. At milepost 6 stay left and follow the road until it ends at the massive trailhead parking area. GPS: N45 16.030' / W117 12.748'

The Hike

Known as the "Oregon Alps," the Wallowa Mountains are worth the price of admission. And in this case the price is 15 miles of hard-breathing, thigh-burning, switchback-laden hiking. This trek into the Eagle Cap Wilderness is justifiably popular. So if you arrive on a summer weekend, prepare to get acquainted with a bunch of fellow nature lovers, as well as horses.

The hike starts out on a wide, rocky dirt path that climbs slowly alongside the west fork of the Wallowa River. After 0.3 mile of hiking you'll reach a junction. If the shorter trip to BC Falls is your goal, turn right onto the Chief Joseph Trail and hike 1 more mile to BC Falls. Then head back the way you came. If, however, Ice Lake is your goal, stay left at the junction with the Chief Joseph Trail.

After close to 3 miles of pleasant hiking, the trail comes to a junction. Stay to the right here and descend down to the river. Take a moment to enjoy the view before crossing a footbridge. After the bridge stay straight. The path soon begins to climb steadily along a set of long, well-graded switchbacks. The hike levels out for a bit

Beauty Falls ▶

Hike to Ice Falls

before arriving at Adam Creek and a second, more arduous set of switchbacks that lead out onto talus slopes. Look for boot paths to the creek and various viewpoints whenever the trail takes a turn near the rushing water. There are no official viewpoints and the trail never really gives a good look at any cascades in this section. Good views can be had of a series of falls in this cluster of switchbacks by going off-trail, but exercise caution.

After leveling off once again, the trail soon arrives at a wide-open and visually stunning basin. And there to greet you is a very visible Beauty Falls. From the same vantage point, the massive Ice Falls can be seen well upstream near the top of the ridge. Continuing past Beauty Falls the trail crosses over a creek and then introduces the toughest test of the day—a dozen or so long, relentless switchbacks. As with the last set, the trail never delivers you to any official views, but boot paths will get you good looks at Ice Falls.

The trail finally levels off near a FIRES PROHIBITED BEYOND THIS POINT sign, which also signifies the end of the heavy lifting hike-wise. The trail continues another half mile, showing off another smaller cascade before finally arriving at a junction just before Ice Lake. To the left, the trail descends down to the creek outlet from the lake where several log crossings are there to help out the cause. From here the trail continues around the lake, where a number of campsites can be found. Alternately, the path to the right leads the opposite way around the lake, skirting the shore before encountering a large meadow and some camping options.

Those interested in even more exercise can take a trail near the meadow an additional 1.5 miles to the summit of the Matterhorn, one of the tallest peaks in eastern Oregon. If you're staying the night, pick a spot. If not, head back the way you came.

Miles and Directions

0.0 From the trailhead, hike 100 feet to a junction. Make a right onto the West Fork Wallowa Trail and continue for 0.3 mile.

Adam Creek Falls

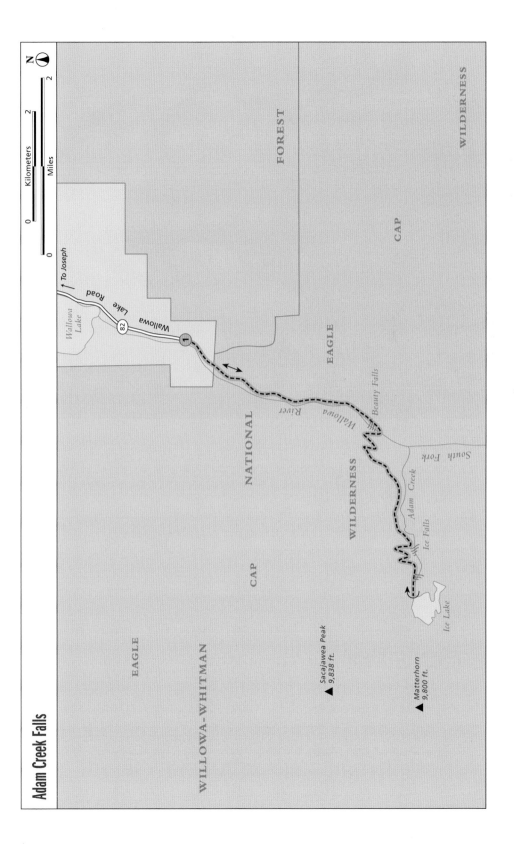

N

Kilometers
0　　　2

Miles
0　　　2

To Joseph

Wallowa Lake

82

Wallowa Lake Road

EAGLE

CAP

WILLOWA-WHITMAN

NATIONAL

FOREST

WILDERNESS

Wallowa River

Beauty Falls

South Fork

Adam Creek

Ice Falls

Ice Lake

Sacajawea Peak
9,838 ft.

Matterhorn
9,800 ft.

EAGLE

CAP

WILDERNESS

The first glimpse of Ice Falls

0.3   Arrive at a T junction. To visit BC Falls, go right and hike 1 mile to the falls. Head back the way you came. To continue to Ice Lake, go left and hike another 2.6 miles to a junction (N45 15.975' / W117 12.992').

2.9   Take the trail to the right, descending to a footbridge across the west fork of the Wallowa River (N45 14.233' / W117 13.815'). Hike for another 4.8 miles to Ice Lake.

7.7   Arrive at Ice Lake. Head back the way you came.

15.4 Arrive back at the trailhead.

WATERFALLS IN WINTER

It's not just flow level and surrounding flora that affect the appearance of waterfalls. When temperatures dip below freezing, the entire area surrounding a waterfall can become quite a scene. I would encourage you to visit your favorite waterfalls in winter. Remember to check road conditions, dress appropriately, and bring traction devices, like Microspikes, for the hike. Here are some examples of waterfalls in summer as compared with winter.

Honorable Mention

A. White River Falls

One of the very best waterfalls in Oregon is also one of the least known and least visited: White River Falls. The two-tiered, 110-foot cascade is jaw-droppingly beautiful and only requires a short but steepish 0.25-mile walk down a dirt path for a complete view of the falls.

To get there from the town of Maupin, head north on US 197 for 9.6 miles. Turn right on OR 216 and drive for 4 more miles to the White River Falls State Park. Park at the signed lot (N45 14.608' / W 121 05.813') near the falls.

White River Falls

Latourell Falls in the summer

Abiqua Falls in the summer

Abiqua Falls in the winter

Latourell Falls in the winter

Columbia River Gorge

Camping and Accommodations

Bridal Veil Lodge: A cozy B&B located on the Historic Columbia River Highway, directly across the street from Bridal Veil Falls. 46650 E. Historic Columbia River Hwy., Corbett, OR 97019; (503) 695-2333; bridalveillodge.com

Columbia Gorge Hotel: This posh hotel in Hood River is home to a renowned restaurant and its own cascade, the massive Wah Gwin Gwin Falls. 4000 State Frontage Rd., Hood River, OR 97031; (541) 386-5566; columbiagorgehotel.com

Ainsworth State Park: Thirty-one sites, $13 to $20 a night. (503) 695-2261
Eagle Creek Campground: Seventeen sites, $10 a night. (541) 308-1700
Wyeth Campground: Fourteen sites, $10 a night. (541) 308-1700

2 Latourell Falls

Latourell Falls is the closest major gorge waterfall to Portland. The 224-foot falls are as powerful and ominous as they are beautiful. The loop hike that visits Latourell and its upper falls is one of the more family-friendly jaunts in the gorge.

Height: Latourell Falls, 224 feet; Upper Latourell Falls, 120 feet
Distance: 2.4-mile loop
Elevation gain: 650 feet
Difficulty: Easy to moderate
Trail surface: Paved, hard-packed dirt, rocky. Wheelchair accessible to Latourell Falls.
Hiking time: About 1–2 hours

County: Multnomah
Land status: State park
Fees and permits: None
Trail contact: Oregon Parks and Recreation Department, (800) 551-6949, oregonstateparks.org
Map: *DeLorme Atlas & Gazetteer Oregon,* page 23, F9

Finding the trailhead: From Portland, take I-84 east to Bridal Veil exit 28. Turn right on the Historic Columbia River Highway (US 30) and travel 2.8 miles to the Latourell parking area on the left. GPS: N45 32.330' / W122 13.061'

The Hike

Latourell is one of the best examples of columnar basalt in the region. The bridge near the bottom of the falls serves as more than just a photo op: It's a great spot to observe visible evidence of the massive basalt lava flows that formed the region. The eroded lava flow that Latourell Creek tumbles over shows off several layers of the honeycombed basalt, as well as unbelievably colored green and orange lichens.

Starting from the parking area, hike up a steep, paved path to a very photo-worthy viewpoint. From here the pavement soon ends and the trail ascends to the top of Latourell Falls. Please avoid the temptation to take any boot paths leading down to the top of the falls. They are dangerous at best.

The hike now joins the creek and the path leads high above lower Latourell to the lesser-visited upper falls. Most visitors pay almost no attention to the 120-foot upper Latourell Falls, a twisting beauty of a cascade. After a creek crossing, the trail ambles through a beautiful bigleaf-maple forest before turning away from the creek. The trail ambles westward with occasional paths to the right leading to semi-obscured gorge views. The trail descends before crossing the historic highway into the enticingly picnic-able Guy W. Talbot State Park. Bear to the right here and pick up the paved path that leads under the Latourell Creek Bridge, bringing you to the base of Latourell Falls before ascending back to the parking area.

Latourell Falls

Latourell Falls

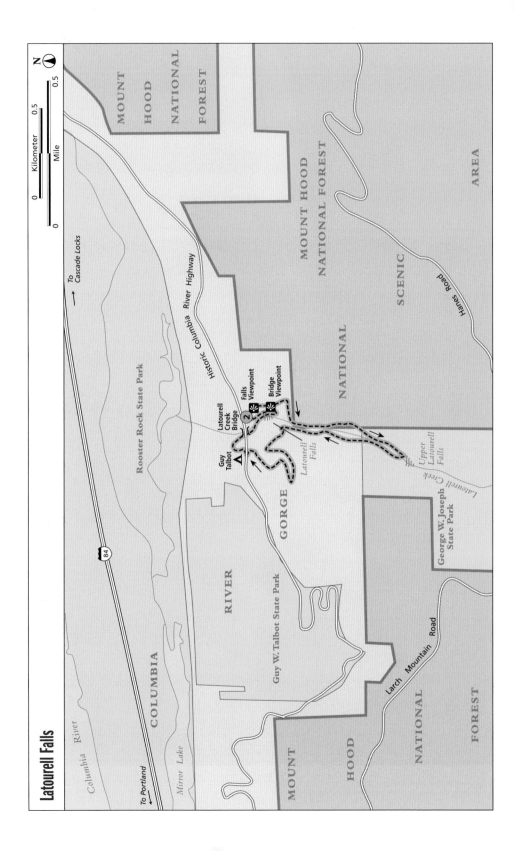

Miles and Directions

0.0 From the parking area, walk up the steep, paved path to a viewing area of Latourell Falls (N45 32.296' / W122 13.056').

0.8 Cross a footbridge at the base of Upper Latourell Falls (N45 31.834' / W122 13.250').

2.1 Carefully cross the Historic Highway and descend a set of steps. Bear right and pick up a paved path leading upstream and under the highway bridge. Cross a footbridge at the base of Latourell Falls (N45 32.248' / W122 13.075') and follow the path back up to the parking area.

2.4 Arrive back at the parking area.

A hiker photographs Latourell Falls.

Bridal Veil Falls

3 Bridal Veil Falls

The Bridal Veil Falls State Scenic Viewpoint sits quietly in the Columbia River Gorge. Located just 15 miles east of Troutdale, the park features restrooms, picnic tables, open grassy areas, and two separate trails. The Overlook Trail loop is a wheelchair-accessible interpretive trail that leads visitors to several stunning gorge views, including Washington's Cape Horn directly across the river. The lower, non-wheelchair-accessible trail drops 0.3 mile down to the 118-foot-tall Bridal Veil Falls.

Height: 118 feet
Distance: 1.0 mile combined out-and-back and loop hikes
Elevation gain: 190 feet
Difficulty: Easy
Trail surface: Paved
Hiking time: About 30 minutes
County: Multnomah

Land status: State park
Fees and permits: None
Trail contact: Oregon Parks and Recreation Department, (800) 551-6949, oregonstateparks.org
Map: *DeLorme Atlas & Gazetteer Oregon,* page 23, F10

Finding the trailhead: From Portland, take I-84 east to Bridal Veil exit 28. Follow the access road for half a mile to the Historic Columbia River Highway. Turn right and proceed 1 mile to the Bridal Veil Falls State Park and its large parking area on the right. GPS: N45 33.218' / W122 10.941'

The Hike

Sitting just off the Historic Columbia River Highway, the Bridal Veil Falls area isn't exactly hidden from site. However, most travelers are on their way to the larger falls, which can be seen directly from the highway. That's not to say that Bridal Veil doesn't get visitors—it most certainly does. But as most of the throngs head toward Multnomah Falls, there is the often overlooked beauty, peace, and interpretive history of Bridal Veil Falls waiting to be enjoyed.

The upper trail provides great views and sign boards that point out the area's unique native plant life. There are also prime picnic spots, tables, and benches along the way. The lower trail ends at the underrated two-tier Bridal Veil Falls.

Miles and Directions

0.0 From the parking area, proceed on the paved trail on the right side of the restrooms toward Bridal Veil Falls.

0.3 Arrive at the Bridal Veil Falls viewing platform (N45 33.298' / W122 10.803'). Head back the way you came.

Bridal Veil Falls, Angel's Rest (Coopey Falls)

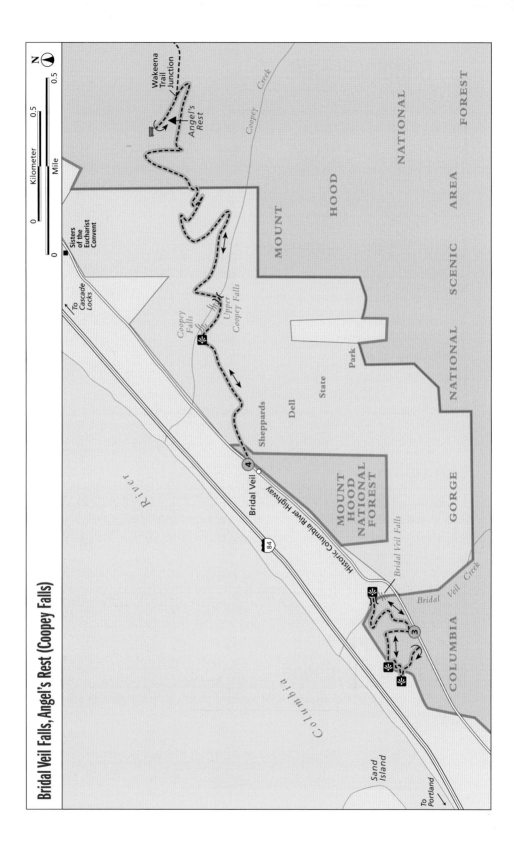

0.6 Arrive back at the trailhead and proceed along the paved path on the left side of the restrooms.

1.0 The paved trail ends at the other end of the parking area.

Train below the Bridal Veil Falls trail

Coopey Falls

4 Angel's Rest (Coopey Falls)

One of the lesser-known and least-visited waterfalls on the Oregon side of the Columbia River Gorge, the top of Coopey Falls is visible from an obscured viewpoint on the Angel's Rest Trail. On this hike the view from atop Angel's Rest is the main attraction, not Coopey Falls. With that stated, however, the 150-foot Coopey Falls and the delicate beauty of the 30-foot Upper Coopey Falls are still well worth a visit for waterfall lovers. Come for the waterfalls, stay for the views.

See map on page 16.
Height: Coopey Falls, 150 feet; Upper Coopey Falls, 30 feet
Distance: 4.5 miles out and back
Elevation gain: 1,500 feet
Difficulty: Moderate
Trail surface: Hard-packed dirt, rocky, areas of talus
Hiking time: About 2-3 hours

County: Multnomah
Land status: National scenic area
Fees and permits: None
Trail contact: Columbia River Gorge National Scenic Area, (541) 308-1700, www.fs.usda.gov/crgnsa
Map: *DeLorme Atlas & Gazetteer Oregon,* page 23, F10

Finding the trailhead: Take I-84 east from Portland to Bridal Veil exit 28, then drive the exit road for 0.5 mile to a junction with the Historic Columbia River Highway. The large, marked Angel's Rest parking area is on the right. The trailhead is across the street from the main parking lot on the south side of the Historic Highway. GPS: N45 33.613' / W122 10.362'

The Hike

You might figure that any hike with an overflow parking area is a popular one, and that most certainly is the case with Angel's Rest. One of the closest gorge hikes from Portland, this is where many an urban hiker can make a quick escape for a good bit of exercise and inspiring views.

This first couple hundred yards of the trail meander through a pleasant forest before ascending across a talus slope. At this point, level sections on the trail will be sparse. Angel's Rest is a good, steady diet of "up." After 0.5 mile of hiking, the trail levels off briefly near the top of Coopey Falls. There are several precarious spots to view the falls from, so exercise caution. Continuing another 100 yards or so, the 30-foot Upper Coopey Falls comes into view just before a footbridge crosses the creek.

The steady ascent continues. After a series of switchbacks, the character of the trail changes noticeably. A 1991 wildfire that swept through the area has left numerous snags, an exposed rockslide, and epic views in its wake. Look for a host of wildflowers in spring and summer, as well as poison oak.

After a final push to the summit, things have the potential to get confusing. Once the trail reaches a ridge crest, it splits to the left and the right. If you're interested in

The hike to Angel's Rest

abandoning ship and heading over to Wahkeena Falls, make a right. If your end goal is Angel's Rest, hang a left. At this point exposure also becomes an issue. After a couple of mindful steps, you will have to make a couple of fairly simple climbing maneuvers to reach the wide-open summit. Take note of where you have ascended and where the trail came from on your way up, as it can be confusing on the way down.

The summit is home to quite a few boot paths that explore the entire area, including one that leads to a nice bench overlooking the Columbia River. There is ample room up here for a picnic, but be forewarned: The notorious Columbia River Gorge winds are often at their most daunting atop Angel's Rest. To complete the hike, head back the way you came.

Note that the best view of Coopey Falls is from the base, which happens to be on the grounds of the Franciscan Sisters of the Eucharist Convent, located a short distance east of the trailhead on the Historic Highway. Not to worry though: If you check in and ask for permission, the sisters are more than happy to let you visit the falls.

Miles and Directions

0.0 The trailhead is across the street from the main parking lot on the south side of the Historic Highway.

0.5 Arrive at the top of Coopey Falls (N45 33.734' W122 09.925').

0.6 Cross a small footbridge over Coopey Creek.

2.25 Arrive at Angel's Rest. Head back the way you came.

4.5 Arrive back at the trailhead.

5 Multnomah/Wahkeena Falls Loop

With combined drops cited at 630 feet, Multnomah Falls is often billed as the tallest waterfall in Oregon. Just up the road from Multnomah Falls is the much less heralded Wahkeena Falls. If Wahkeena were located anywhere else in Oregon, it would be a stand-alone attraction. What you miss from the road, however, is everything above both of these falls. As it happens, you can visit both falls, as well as four other named cascades, by hiking the classic Multnomah/Wahkeena Falls loop.

Height: Multnomah Falls, 630 feet (combined drops); Wahkeena Falls, 242 feet; Fairy Falls, 20 feet; Ecola Falls, 55 feet; Weisendanger Falls, 50 feet; Dutchman Falls, 35 feet
Distance: 5.6-mile loop hike
Elevation gain: 1,650 feet
Difficulty: Moderate
Trail surface: Paved, hard-packed dirt, rocky
Hiking time: About 2–4 hours

County: Multnomah
Land status: National scenic area
Fees and permits: None
Trail contact: Columbia River Gorge National Scenic Area, (541) 308-1700, www.fs.usda.gov/crgnsa
Map: *DeLorme Atlas & Gazetteer Oregon*, page 23, F10

Finding the trailhead: To get there, take I-84 east from Portland to Multnomah Falls exit 31. Find parking where you can and walk through the tunnel to the historic Multnomah Falls Lodge. Walk west past the lodge on the south side of the Historic Highway about 100 feet to the clearly marked trailhead leading toward Wahkeena Falls. GPS: N45 34.676' / W122 07.189'

The Hike

Yes, there are crowds most of the year, but it never gets old seeing the expression on a visiting face the first time it witnesses Multnomah Falls. Embrace it. Enjoy the giant ice cream cookie thingy and a cup of coffee at the end of the hike. Eat a hot dog or have a sit-down dinner at the lodge and listen to others marvel over what they've just seen. Sure it's a mob scene close to the falls, but as is the case with many trails in the area, once the pavement ends the crowds thin out considerably.

Starting the hike by walking away from Multnomah Falls is a bit like eating breakfast before opening presents on Christmas morning, but that's what I'm recommending here. Start at the Multnomah Falls Lodge and head west along the Historic Highway. A short distance from the lodge, pick up the marked trail to Wahkeena Falls. There isn't much to this part of the trail, which is why it's good to start here; plus it's a nice warm-up.

Cross a footbridge at Wahkeena Falls and continue up along a paved path. You soon come to a stone bridge that crosses the creek within spraying distance of the

Multnomah Falls

Multnomah Falls in fall

falls. Continue up some long, steep, switchbacks to Lemmon's Viewpoint. Enjoy the view and catch your breath before heading up the Wahkeena Canyon along the now-unpaved path. The trail marches up through the scenic canyon before arriving at the small but beautiful Fairy Falls. Hike past the falls a short distance to a junction with the Vista Point Trail. Stay right, and continue on the Wahkeena Trail. At the next junction it's worth taking a right onto the Angel's Rest Trail for about 100 yards to visit Wahkeena Springs. The spot where Wahkeena Creek emerges from the ground also makes an excellent rest stop. When you're ready, go back to the Wahkeena Trail and make one last push to the top of the ridge and the end of the climbing.

At the four-way junction, stay straight, passing the steep ascent to Devil's Rest on the right. Follow the now-level trail for 1 mile before it descends to a junction with the Larch Mountain Trail. Turn left here and follow Multnomah Creek as it passes Ecola, Weisendanger, and Dutchman Falls on its way to a small bridge crossing. Just after the crossing, the pavement begins again and meets a two-way junction. Take the short jaunt to the left to visit the viewing platform at the top of Multnomah Falls. Return to the main path and ascend briefly before beginning the paved mile-long descent to the base of Multnomah Falls and the end of the hike.

Multnomah/Wahkeena Falls Loop

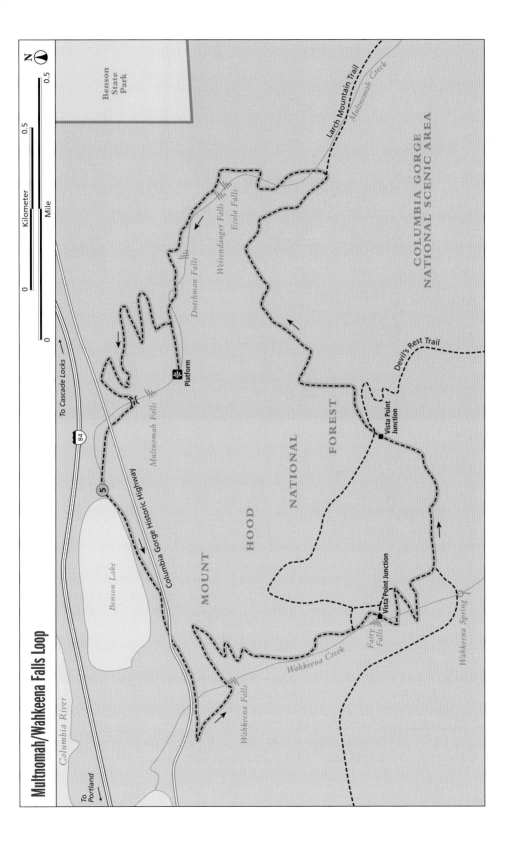

N

Kilometer

0   0.5   0.5

0   0.5   Mile

Columbia River

To Portland

To Cascade Locks

84

5

Benson Lake

Columbia Gorge Historic Highway

Multnomah Falls

Platform

Dutchman Falls

Weisendanger Falls

Ecola Falls

Larch Mountain Trail

Multnomah Creek

Benson State Park

COLUMBIA GORGE NATIONAL SCENIC AREA

MOUNT   HOOD   NATIONAL   FOREST

Devil's Rest Trail

Vista Point Junction

Vista Point Junction

Fairy Falls

Wahkeena Creek

Wahkeena Spring

Wahkeena Falls

The hike between Wahkeena and Multnomah Falls

Miles and Directions

0.0 From the Multnomah Falls Lodge, head west along the Historic Highway and pick up the marked trail to Wahkeena Falls.

0.3 Arrive at the Wahkeena Falls Trailhead. Continue up the paved path.

0.6 Arrive at Wahkeena Falls Bridge. Continue up the paved path.

2.3 Continue up switchbacks to Lemmon's Viewpoint (N45 34.445' / W122 07.600'). Paved trail ends. Hike up along Wahkeena Creek, passing Fairy Falls (N45 34.215' / W122 07.481') and a junction with the Vista Point Trail, arriving at a junction with the Angel's Rest Trail. Take a right, and arrive a short time later at Wahkeena Springs. Head back to the junction.

3.4 Continue east on the Wahkeena Trail and past a junction leading to Devil's Rest, arriving at a junction with the Larch Mountain Trail.

4.1 Make a left at the junction and head downstream following Multnomah Creek. Pass Ecola (N45 34.455' / W122 06.437'), Weisendanger (N45 34.491' / W122 06.474'), and Dutchman Falls (N45 34.552' / W122 06.597') before crossing a small footbridge and arriving at a junction leading to the Multnomah Falls viewing platform. If you would like to see the falls from above, walk down to the platform. Otherwise, stay right.

5.6 Descend several paved switchbacks, cross the Benson Bridge at Multnomah Falls (N45 34.603' / W122 06.984'), and arrive back at the lodge.

6 Oneonta Gorge

This little adventure is indeed one-of-a-kind. The Oneonta Gorge is a slot canyon barely 0.6 mile long in the Columbia River Gorge. Designated a botanical area by the US Forest Service, the steep basalt walls of the canyon are home to numerous rare plants and an incredibly scenic waterfall. At just over a mile round-trip, this hike doesn't set any distance records, but burning lungs and thigh muscles aren't why people visit this falls.

Height: Lower Oneonta Falls, 100 feet
Distance: 1.2 miles out and back
Elevation gain: 70 feet
Difficulty: Moderate
Trail surface: Creek bed, water, rocky
Hiking time: About 1–2 hours
County: Multnomah

Land status: National scenic area
Fees and permits: None
Trail contact: Columbia River Gorge National Scenic Area, (541) 308-1700, www.fs.usda.gov/crgnsa
Map: *DeLorme Atlas & Gazetteer Oregon*, page 24, F1

Finding the trailhead: To get there, take I-84 east to exit 35 and follow the Historic Highway 2 miles to a parking area just past the recently reopened Oneonta Tunnel. Walk down a set of stairs located just before the bridge and begin making your way upstream. GPS: N45 35.372' / W122 04.534'

The Hike

The moment you descend the staircase leading to the Oneonta Creek, you're welcomed with an air temperature that can be as much as twenty degrees cooler than where you parked. There may be no better place in the Columbia River Gorge on a hot summer day! The cool canyon is narrow, with 100-foot walls of rock on either side. First things first, however, you have to get up, over, or around a large logjam that changes with each season. Exercise caution here and gauge your hiking party's abilities. Though children frequently make this journey under the watchful eye of parents, this is very much a personal judgment call. Once the jam has been negotiated, the actual journey begins. Don't bother looking for a trail here—Oneonta Creek is the trail.

This is definitely a warm weather endeavor. The water in the shaded creek is cold and ranges from ankle deep to chest high. Good water shoes, a bathing suit, and the love of cold mountain water are definitely recommended. Now that you've been sufficiently scared, most folks make it out and back without issue.

Shortly after the deepest wading, the 100-foot-high Lower Oneonta Falls emerges from around a corner. The falls are long and elegant, with an invitingly swimmable splash pool. This area can become crowded on hot summer weekends, but having this grotto to yourself on a weekday is magical.

Oneonta Gorge, Horsetail Falls/Triple Falls Loop

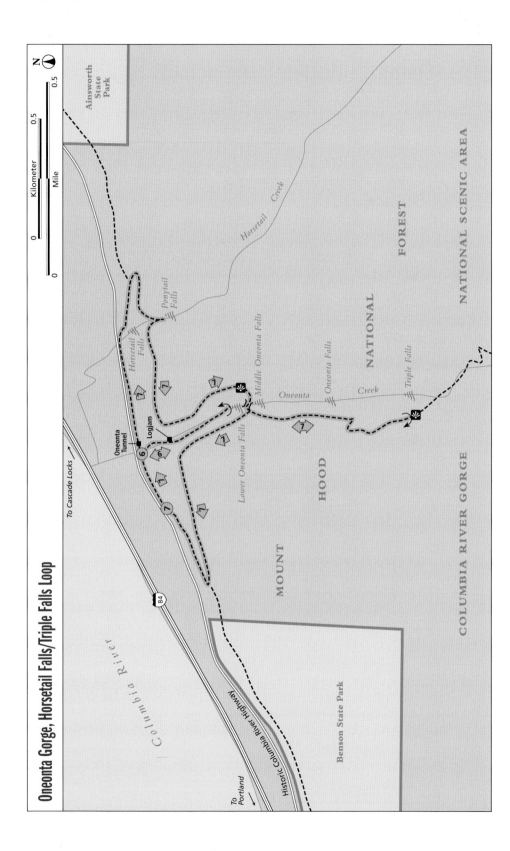

Lower Oneonta Falls

Miles and Directions

0.0   Begin by walking down the staircase at the west end of the Oneonta Creek Bridge. Proceed upstream and over the logjam. Continue creek walking and wading upstream.

0.6   Arrive at the base of Lower Oneonta Falls (N45 35.181' / W122 04.379'). Head back the way you came.

1.2   Arrive at the trailhead.

7 Horsetail Falls/Triple Falls Loop

The Horsetail to Triple Falls semi-loop is yet another classic Columbia River Gorge day hike. One of the more popular stops on the Oregon side of the gorge, the Horsetail Falls parking lot fills quickly during the warm summer months. Though the hike is indeed very popular, most people are here to take a picture or two of the roadside falls and move on.

See map on page 28.
Height: Horsetail Falls, 214 feet; Ponytail Falls, 88 feet; Middle Oneonta Falls, 24 feet; Triple Falls, 64 feet
Distance: 4.5-mile semi-loop
Elevation gain: 1,050 feet
Difficulty: Moderate
Trail surface: Hard-packed dirt, rocky
Hiking time: About 1.5–3 hours

County: Multnomah
Land status: National scenic area
Fees and permits: None
Trail contact: Columbia River Gorge National Scenic Area, (541) 308-1700, www.fs.usda .gov/crgnsa
Map: *DeLorme Atlas & Gazetteer Oregon,* page 24, F1

Finding the trailhead: From Portland, take I-84 east to Ainsworth Park exit 35. Take the Historic Columbia River Highway west for 1.5 miles to the Horsetail Falls Trailhead parking area. The trail begins on the left side of the falls. GPS: N45 35.405' / W122 04.096'

The Hike

If you enjoy hiking in the Columbia River Gorge, this trip exemplifies every reason for that. There are numerous waterfalls to take in, including one you can walk behind. In winter licorice ferns sprout from the mosses that cling to bigleaf maple trees, and photographers are drawn to capture infinite patterns of frozen spray and glassy stones created in the splash pool of Horsetail Falls. And last but not least, there are trademark gorge views stretching across the river to Beacon Rock and beyond.

After 0.2 mile stay right on the Gorge Trail as it steadily makes its way above Horsetail Falls. The trail soon turns a corner and arrives at Ponytail Falls. The path enters a grotto behind the falls before ascending again. Hike another 0.4 mile. Just before the main trail turns left into the canyon of Oneonta Creek, look for unmarked trails that spur off to the right. These boot paths lead to good views of the gorge.

The main trail now skirts along the east side of the Oneonta Gorge before switch-backing down to the creek and a footbridge next to 24-foot Middle Oneonta Falls. After two short switchbacks you come to the junction leading to Triple Falls. Turn left here and travel the 0.9 mile to the viewpoint of Triple Falls. Beyond the view-point is a footbridge with good lunch spots on either side. For waterfall aficionados,

Triple Falls

The Horsetail Falls Trailhead in fall

one of the best reasons to hike this trail is to visit Triple Falls. The unique falls splits into three cascading segments before reconvening at the base.

Head back the 0.9 mile to the trail junction and stay straight this time, following the Oneonta Trail until it reaches the Historic Highway. Turn right (east) and walk along the road for 0.5 mile back to the parking area. Take care here, as the road's shoulder is narrow in spots. Along the way, take time to visit the recently restored Oneonta Tunnel. Reopened in 2009, the historic passageway is now open to foot traffic.

Miles and Directions

0.0 From the parking area, walk across the street and down the steps to visit Horsetail Falls (N45 35.405' / W122 04.096'). Walk back up the steps and begin hiking from the trailhead on the east side of Horsetail Falls.

0.2 Arrive at a junction with the Gorge Trail, make a right and continue up to and behind Ponytail Falls (N45 35.356' / W122 04.125'). Proceed past a couple of gorge viewpoints and down a set of switchbacks that lead over a footbridge that looks down at the top of Lower

Oneonta Falls. On the other end of the bridge is a viewpoint of Middle Oneonta Falls (N45 35.108' / W122 04.369'). Continue up the trail.

1.3 Arrive at a junction with the Oneonta Trail. Turn left toward Triple Falls.

2.2 Arrive at the viewpoint for Triple Falls (N45 34.758' / W122 04.333'). Hike back the way you came.

3.1 Arrive back at a trail junction. Continue straight here, staying on the Oneonta Trail—do not go back down toward the footbridge. The trail soon descends down to the Historic Highway.

4.0 Arrive at the Historic Highway. Make a right and walk back east along the shoulder of the highway, passing the historic, restored Oneonta Tunnel on the way.

4.5 Arrive back at the parking area.

Hiking behind Ponytail Falls

8 Elowah/Upper McCord Creek Falls

One of many projects completed by the Civilian Conservation Corps in the 1930s, the McCord Creek Trail leads up to a pair of the Columbia River Gorge's most dramatic, accessible, and yet somehow lesser-known waterfalls. The lower section of the trail visits the 213-foot Elowah Falls and its mossy, boulder-filled amphitheater. A fork in the trail ascends to Upper McCord Creek Falls, a photogenic 64-foot twin cascade.

Height: Elowah Falls, 213 feet; Upper McCord Creek Falls, 64 feet
Distance: 3.0 miles combined
Elevation gain: 700 feet
Difficulty: Easy to moderate
Trail surface: Hard-packed dirt, rocky
Hiking time: About 1.5-2.5 hours
County: Multnomah

Land status: State park
Fees and permits: Northwest Forest Pass or small day-use fee required
Trail contact: Oregon Parks and Recreation Department, (800) 551-6949, oregonstate parks.org
Map: *DeLorme Atlas & Gazetteer Oregon,* page 24, E1-E2

Finding the trailhead: From Portland, take I-84 east to exit 35. Turn left, following signs for Dodson. After 150 feet turn right onto the frontage road and drive 2 miles to the trailhead parking area on the right. GPS: N45 36.747' / W122 00.281'

The Hike

If you're bringing younger kids, you might want to consider just taking the lower trail to Elowah Falls. The easy 1.5-mile round-trip hike to Elowah ranks high on the "bang for the buck" scale. This is also a great spot to hit in winter because water levels are robust and the low elevation of the falls ensures the trail is usually free of snow and ice.

The side trail leading to Upper McCord Creek Falls is memorable for many reasons. It doesn't add a whole lot of distance, but the Civilian Conservation Corps blasted portions of this upper trail out along basalt cliffs. The result is a trail with stunning views but also some exposure. There's a handrail for some of the dicier locations, and if it's within your comfort level, you'll be treated to some excellent views of Beacon Rock and Hamilton Mountain. Above the creek are easily discernible layers of basalt. Each layer is millions of years old and a reminder of the lava flows that helped form the region.

If you combine both trails into one outing you get two world-class waterfalls in a tidy 3.0-mile, 700-foot-elevation-gain hike.

From the trailhead, start at the west end of the parking area and walk past an old water tank to a junction with the trail to Nesmith Point. Stay left for 0.8 mile

Elowah Falls

Elowah/Upper McCord Creek Falls

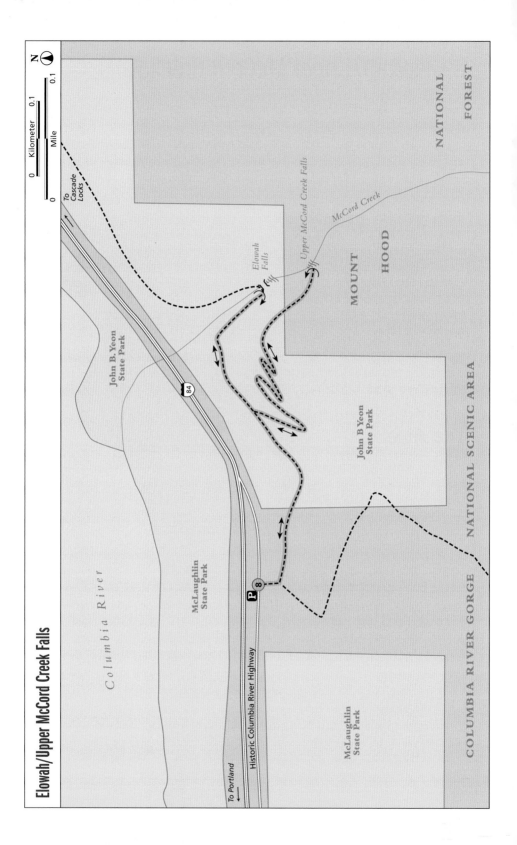

Trail to upper McCord Creek Falls

until you reach Elowah Falls. Backtrack 0.5 mile and take a left at a fork. Follow the switchbacks and blasted-out trail to Upper McCord Creek Falls. The trail ends a short way past the falls. Head back the way you came.

Miles and Directions

0.0 From the trailhead on the west side of the parking area, hike past a water tower and stay left at the junction for Nesmith Point. Go past a junction for the upper trail, continuing east and eventually descending down to McCord Creek.

0.8 Arrive at Elowah Falls (N45 36.773' / W121 59.688'). Hike back the way you came.

1.2 Arrive back at the junction with the upper trail and bear left. The trail ascends to a railed section of trail before arriving at the Upper McCord Creek Falls Viewpoint (N45 36.736' / W121 59.696').

1.9 Arrive at the Upper McCord Creek Falls Viewpoint. Backtrack to the junction with the lower trail and go left, returning to the parking area.

3.0 Arrive back at the trailhead.

9 Wahclella Falls

Wahclella Falls receives far fewer visitors than the average Columbia River Gorge waterfall, perhaps due to lack of stature and visibility, as well as length of hike. The second and most visible 60-foot drop of the falls occupies a peaceful grotto at the end of a deep canyon. Although hikers feeling the need for more exercise often overlook it, Wahclella rates as high as any hike in the area in terms of beauty, if not distance.

Height: Wahclella Falls (combined drops), 127 feet; Munra Falls, 68 feet
Distance: 2.0-mile semi-loop
Elevation gain: 400 feet
Difficulty: Easy
Trail surface: Gravel, hard-packed dirt, rocky
Hiking time: About 1–2 hours
County: Multnomah

Land status: State park
Fees and permits: Northwest Forest Pass or small day-use fee required
Trail contact: Oregon Parks and Recreation Department, (800) 551-6949, oregonstate parks.org
Map: *DeLorme Atlas & Gazetteer Oregon,* page 24, E2

Finding the trailhead: To access the trailhead, take I-84 east to the Bonneville Dam exit 40. Turn right and go 100 yards to the turnaround and parking area. There is a small day-use fee if you don't have a Northwest Forest Pass. GPS: N45 37.817' / W121 57.235'

The Hike

This easy semi-loop allows hikers of almost any age and aptitude the opportunity to explore and enjoy the canyon's many attributes. The trail starts alongside Tanner Creek on a roadbed until it ends near a small dam that diverts water to a fish hatchery downstream. From here the trail begins to head upstream, but not before a bridge takes you within arm's reach of another 68-foot waterfall, Munra Falls. Munra looks as much like a water-park slide as it does a naturally occurring cascade, and it will often give you a light misting in late winter and spring.

The trail forks around the 0.8-mile mark. Either direction will lead to the falls, but take the trail to the right that descends back down to the creek and a long wooden bridge. This is a great spot to observe the gigantic boulders that re-formed the creek after a landslide in 1973. The building-size obstructions created a series of mini-falls and pools.

Continuing upstream, the sound of Wahclella can soon be heard echoing through the canyon, and you'll catch your first glimpse of the falls soon after. Now the area opens up and becomes endlessly explorable. There are boulders to climb and small pools to wade through. Be mindful, however, that this is still a dangerously fast-moving creek in spots. There is even a mini-cave just before a bridge that recrosses the creek on its way to the falls. You can't go back too far, but younger hikers often

Wahclella Falls

refuse to pass by without inspecting the darkness. After the bridge the trail leads up to a rocky viewpoint of the falls. While the main tier of the falls is only 60 feet high, the water is forced out of a narrow slot that produces an impressive thundering water-hose effect. From here, follow the convoluted trail on the east side of the creek back downstream to the trailhead.

Miles and Directions

0.0　From the trailhead, head upstream on a wide gravel road. Continue past a water intake dam and cross a footbridge next to Munra Falls (N45 37.575' / W121 57.208'). Proceed along the trail to a junction.

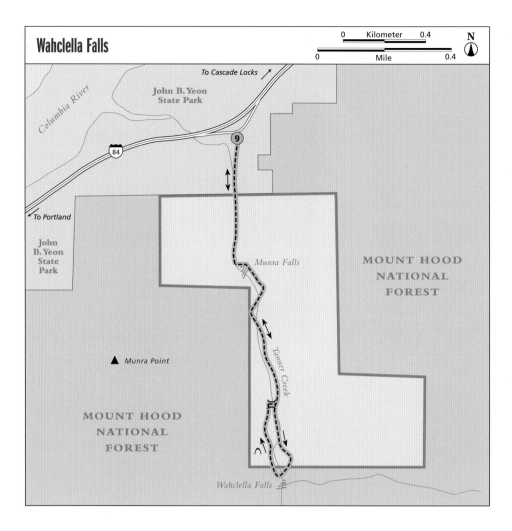

0   Kilometer   0.4

0   Mile   0.4

N

To Cascade Locks

John B. Yeon
State Park

84

9

To Portland

John
B. Yeon
State
Park

Columbia River

Munra Falls

MOUNT HOOD
NATIONAL
FOREST

▲ Munra Point

Tanner Creek

MOUNT HOOD
NATIONAL
FOREST

Wahclella Falls

0.8   Either route will lead to the falls before looping back to the junction. For navigational purposes, bear right and descend down to a long footbridge crossing Tanner Creek. Continue along the trail, crossing another bridge before arriving at Wahclella Falls.

1.0   Arrive at Wahclella Falls (N45 37.104' / W121 57.084'). The trail leads up to the falls and then ascends the canyon wall, heading downstream on the east side of Tanner Creek. Stay straight at the trail junction and continue back to the trailhead.

2.0   Arrive back at the trailhead.

10 Eagle Creek

Built in 1915, the Eagle Creek Trail opened in conjunction with the Historic Columbia River Highway. The trail leads through one of the most sensational canyons in the entire Columbia Gorge. Along the way you'll travel a path that was blasted out of basalt cliffs, visit numerous waterfalls, and cross bridges that offer spectacular views of chasms below. The trail is well kept, often wide, and gently graded, making it a great option for novices. There are, however, a couple of sections where the trail is narrow and exposed. Cabling is provided in these sections to help ease your mind, but you still might want to proceed with caution.

Height: Metlako Falls, 82 feet; Lower Punchbowl Falls, 12 feet; Punchbowl Falls, 36 feet; Loowit Falls, 60 feet; Tunnel Falls, 130 feet; Twister Falls, 140 feet; 7 Mile Falls, 50 feet
Distance: 4.2 miles out and back to Punchbowl Falls, 12.5 miles out and back to Tunnel Falls, 13.5 miles out and back to 7 Mile Falls
Elevation gain: 400 feet (Punchbowl), 1,450 feet (Tunnel), 1,700 feet (7 Mile)
Difficulty: Easy to difficult
Trail surface: Hard-packed dirt, rocky

Hiking time: About 2–8 hours
County: Hood River
Land status: State park
Fees and permits: Northwest Forest Pass or small day-use fee required
Trail contact: Oregon Parks and Recreation Department, (800) 551-6949, oregonstate parks.org
Map: DeLorme Atlas & Gazetteer Oregon, page 24, E2

Finding the trailhead: To get there, take I-84 east to exit 41 and turn right at the bottom of the exit. Travel 0.6 mile along a narrow road to the parking area and trailhead (GPS: N45 38.208' / W121 55.175'). If that parking area is full, park back at the parking area near the front of the park. As an added bonus, October and November are prime times to watch salmon making their way upstream to spawn. Eagle Creek is one of the premier spots in the Columbia River Gorge to witness this marvel of nature. Some of the best viewing is available at the trailhead and along the creek's first stretch of hiking.

The Hike

As with any out-and-back hike, you have options with regard to how long you would like your outing to be. And based on how tired or spry you're feeling, you can always call an audible. The three recommended options are a 4.2-mile stroll up to Punchbowl Falls, a 12.5-mile hike to Tunnel Falls, or a 13.5-mile trek to 7 Mile Falls. You can take 0.5 mile off of the last two options if you cut out the side trips to Metlako and Punchbowl.

From the trailhead, hike 1.5 miles to a junction with a side trail on the right leading down to a viewpoint of Metlako Falls. After the falls, continue another 0.3 mile along the main path to the junction with the Lower Punchbowl Trail. Take this trail

Tunnel Falls

down 0.25 mile to Punchbowl Falls and Lower Punchbowl Falls. This is the turn-around point for the 4.2-mile hike option.

To get to Tunnel Falls, return to the main path and continue to High Bridge. From there, hike another 2.75 miles, passing several nice lunch spots and small, scenic cascades before arriving at Tunnel Falls. This one-of-a-kind 120-foot cascade features a tunnel chipped through solid rock that goes behind the falls.

In addition to bonus waterfalls, this final 0.5-mile stretch is some of the most scenic of the hike. Just 0.25 mile past Tunnel Falls waits the aptly named Twister Falls. Another 0.25 mile later you'll arrive at 7 Mile Falls and the official turnaround point. Head back the way you came.

Miles and Directions

0.0 From the trailhead, follow the trail up the east side of Eagle Creek. Look for a spur trail (N45 37.627' / W121 53.816') to the Metlako Falls viewpoint (N45 37.637' / W121 53.856') at the 1.6-mile mark.

1.8 Arrive at a junction with the Lower Punchbowl Trail. Make a right here and hike steeply down to the water and Lower Punchbowl Falls (N45 37.382' / W121 53.716') and a

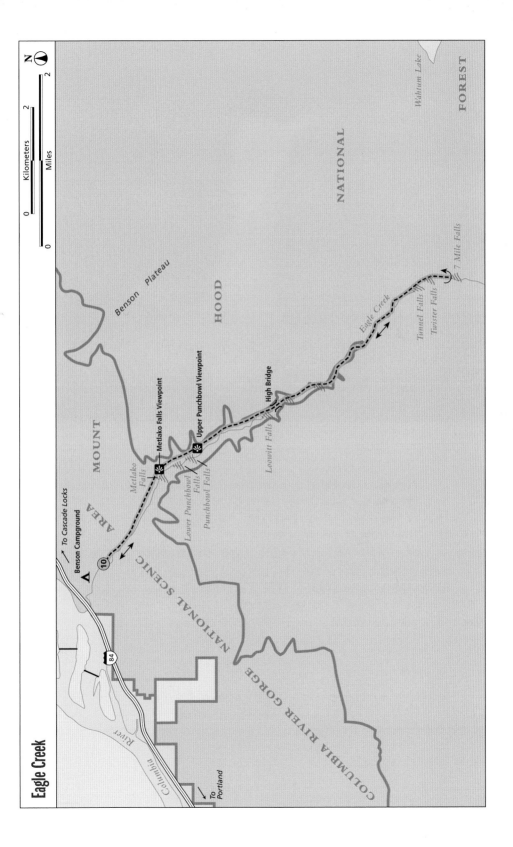

Eagle Creek

N

0   2   Kilometers
0   2   Miles

To Portland

Columbia River

84

To Cascade Locks

Benson Campground

10

MOUNT

AREA

Benson Plateau

HOOD

NATIONAL

FOREST

Wahtum Lake

COLUMBIA RIVER GORGE NATIONAL SCENIC

Metlako Falls

Metlako Falls Viewpoint

Lower Punchbowl Falls

Punchbowl Falls

Upper Punchbowl Viewpoint

High Bridge

Loowitt Falls

Eagle Creek

Tunnel Falls

Twister Falls

7 Mile Falls

Punchbowl Falls

view of Punchbowl Falls (N45 37.340' / W121 53.677'). Back at the main trail, continue to the right, passing an upper viewpoint for Punchbowl Falls as well as Loowit Falls (N45 36.522' / W121 53.073') just before arriving at High Bridge.

3.5   Arrive at High Bridge. Continue along the trail.

6.25   Arrive at Tunnel Falls (N45 35.118' / W121 51.140'). Continue another 0.25 mile to Twister Falls (N45 34.922' / W121 51.161').

6.5   Arrive at Twister Falls. Continue 0.25 mile to 7 Mile Falls (N45 34.692' / W121 51.128').

6.75   Arrive at 7 Mile Falls. Head back the way you came.

13.5   Arrive back at the trailhead.

11 Dry Creek Falls

Contrary to its name, Dry Creek Falls flows steadily all year long. From the Bridge of the Gods Trailhead in Cascade Locks, hikers follow the final stretch of the Oregon portion of the Pacific Crest Trail to a lightly visited 75-foot waterfall.

Height: 75 feet
Distance: 4.2 miles out and back
Elevation gain: 650 feet
Difficulty: Moderate
Trail surface: Hard-packed dirt, rocky
Hiking time: About 2–3 hours
County: Hood River
Land status: National scenic area

Fees and permits: Northwest Forest Pass or small day-use fee required
Trail contact: Columbia River Gorge National Scenic Area, (541) 308-1700, www.fs.usda .gov/crgnsa
Map: *DeLorme Atlas & Gazetteer Oregon,* page 24, E3

Finding the trailhead: Take I-84 east to Cascade Locks exit 44. Turn right toward the Bridge of the Gods and park in the area designated for the trailhead on the right. GPS: N45 39.715' / W121 53.782'

The Hike

The Pacific Crest Trail's (PCT) home stretch in Oregon is a lush, forested trail that sees mostly thru-hikers during the summer months. Though wonderfully scenic, the rest of the year, the trail rarely entertains visitors compared to other waterfall trails in the Columbia River Gorge. Thus, this hike is a good one for avoiding crowds.

In addition to the allure of solitude, the forest leading to the falls has a good blend of maples strewn throughout, providing color in fall. And while many gorge waterfalls are awe-inspiring, thunderous cascades that keep visitors well back, Dry Creek Falls offers all the visual beauty with accessibility. In fact,

The trail to Dry Creek Falls in fall

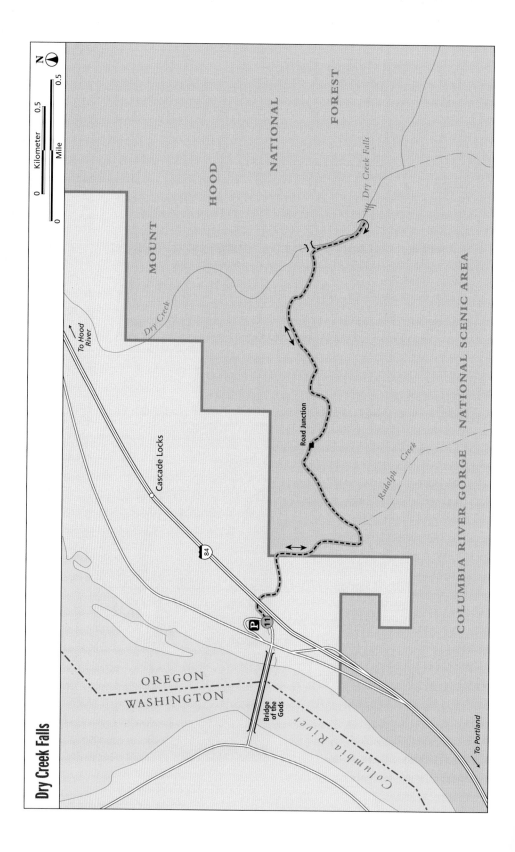

Dry Creek Falls

MOUNT

HOOD

NATIONAL

FOREST

Dry Creek Falls

Dry Creek

To Hood
River

Road Junction

Rudolph Creek

Cascade Locks

84

11

P

OREGON

WASHINGTON

Bridge
of the
Gods

Columbia River

To Portland

COLUMBIA RIVER GORGE   NATIONAL SCENIC AREA

Dry Creek Falls

the remnants of an old dam structure allow you to cross the creek and approach the falls quite easily.

Miles and Directions

0.0 From the trailhead restrooms, cross to the south side of the bridge access road. Follow the trail up the bank until it meets with a paved road that goes under the freeway. Bear right after the freeway onto a narrow gravel road that travels 75 yards to a trail junction. Head left here onto the PCT.

0.5 The trail intersects with a gravel road. Go up this road for 50 yards before the trail splits off to the left again. Follow the trail for another 1.4 miles until it reaches a dirt road.

1.9 Arrive at a dirt road. Make a right here but do not cross the bridge going over Dry Creek. Continue up this road for the last 0.2 mile to Dry Creek Falls (N45 39.435' / W121 52.037').

2.1 Arrive at the falls. Below the falls the remains of an old water-diversion dam are worth inspecting and actually aid in crossing Dry Creek for close-up photo ops. Head back the way you came.

4.2 Arrive back at the trailhead.

Starvation Creek Falls

12 Starvation Creek Falls

Starvation Creek Falls is a towering 227-foot waterfall with a developed viewing area and picnic tables. It's a stately waterfall in and of itself, but there are also three other waterfalls in the vicinity that can all be visited by taking a wonderfully diverse loop hike. The area is also home to some interesting Columbia River Gorge history.

Height: Starvation Creek Falls, 227 feet; Lancaster Falls, 303 feet (combined drops, last drop 20 feet); Hole-in-the-Wall Falls, 96 feet; Cabin Creek Falls, 220 feet (combined drops)
Distance: 2.5-mile loop
Elevation gain: 800 feet
Difficulty: Easy to moderate
Trail surface: Hard-packed dirt, rocky, paved sections

Hiking time: About 1.5-3 hours
County: Hood River
Land status: State park
Fees and permits: None
Trail contact: Oregon Parks and Recreation Department, (800) 551-6949, oregonstate parks.org
Map: DeLorme Atlas & Gazetteer Oregon, page 24, E4

Finding the trailhead: From Portland, take I-84 east to exit 55, which quickly dead-ends at the parking area. If coming from Hood River, take exit 51, turn around, and drive back to exit 55. GPS: N45 41.292' / W121 41.452'

The Hike

The creek was originally named "Starveout Creek" due to an incident in 1884 when two trains were stranded by a blizzard in the area for two weeks. It all ended well, however, as nobody actually starved or died in the incident.

Later, in 1939, the highway department constructed a massive metal weir and tunnel system to divert water from the top of what was once Warren Falls, through a massive basalt cliff to where it now spits out as Hole-in-the-Wall Falls.

The reason for all of this rather impressive engineering was because water and debris from Warren Falls was causing trouble for the newly constructed Historic Highway. So instead of rerouting the road, they rerouted the waterfall. At the time this guide was published, ODOT was in the process of a rather large-scale Historic Highway restoration project. There is a grassroots push to have Warren Falls restored in the process. If you're interested in the cause, there is a Facebook page, www.face book.com/RestoreWarrenFalls.

To visit Starvation Creek Falls, walk along a paved path to the right of the restrooms. Follow the path upstream a short way to the viewing area. To take the loop hike, walk back toward the freeway exit you took to get to the parking area and walk west along the shoulder of the road. Eventually the trail dips down into the woods, following a segment of the Historic Highway. After 0.2 mile you will reach an easy-to-miss junction with the Starvation Cutoff Trail on your left. The Cutoff Trail

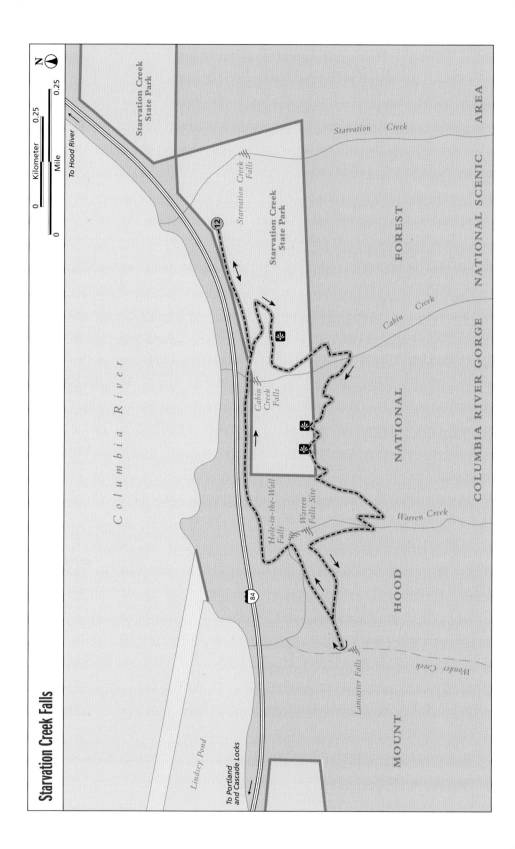

Starvation Creek Falls

is steep—really steep—potentially causing you to use your hands in a couple of spots kind of steep. But it's better to go up it than come down it, so up you go.

After 0.5 mile of lung-burning climbing, you'll arrive at a junction with the Starvation Creek Trail; make a right here. The next mile of hiking visits viewpoints, hanging meadows, and creek crossings before arriving at a junction with the Mount Defiance Trail. Continue to the left along this trail, but only for 100 yards or so until you reach the bottom of Lancaster Falls. Then, head back to the junction and proceed down to the left, across a rock slope, before reentering the trees.

The trail now levels out, passing Hole-in-the-Wall Falls

An Oregon Field Guide *film crew stands at the base of what once was Warren Falls.*

and a footbridge over Warren Creek. If you're interested in visiting what used to be Warren Falls, leave the trail and scramble up the dry creek bed, around a corner, and up into the beautiful basalt amphitheater that was once home to Warren Falls. Once back on the main trail, continue east, past Cabin Creek Falls and back to the parking area.

Miles and Directions

0.0 Walk back toward the freeway exit heading west along the shoulder of the road. Follow the trail into the woods.

0.2 Take the Starvation Cutoff Trail to the left.

0.7 Arrive at a junction with the Starvation Creek Trail. Make a right here.

1.7 Arrive at a junction with the Mount Defiance Trail. Continue to the left to Lancaster Falls (N45 41.098' / W121 42.362'). Head back to the junction and proceed down to the left, passing Hole-in-the-Wall Falls (N45 41.178' / W121 42.131'), a dry Warren Falls (N45 41.176' / W121 42.100'), and Cabin Creek Falls (N45 41.243' / W121 41.784') on the way back to the parking area.

2.5 Arrive back at the trailhead.

Honorable Mentions

B. Shepperd's Dell

In 1915 dairy farmer George Shepperd donated his land to the city of Portland as a memorial to his wife. The multitiered Shepperd's Dell Falls tumbles a total of 220 feet within the donated parcel of land.

To visit the falls from Portland, take I-84 east to exit 28. Merge onto Bridal Veil Road and after 0.2 mile make a sharp right onto the Historic Columbia River Highway. Drive 1.6 more miles to a pullout just before a bridge. Take the staircase at the signed Shepperd's Dell a short way down to the falls (N45 32.865' / W122 11.776').

C. Mist Falls

Mist Falls is the tall, windblown, wispy falls easily seen from I-84 about 1 mile west of Multnomah Falls. Contrary to popular belief, the falls are not seasonal, though they are reduced to an exaggerated trickle at times during the summer. A short but sweet scramble leads to the base of the falls. Perhaps the most interesting thing about the area, however, is the remains of the old Multnomah Lodge. What was sometimes referred to as the Mist Lodge, the roadhouse burned down in 1929, but the fireplace and chimney still stand near the beginning of the boot path.

To visit the falls from Portland, take I-84 east to exit 28. Turn left and head east along the Historic Highway. Just past milepost 31 there is a small pullout on the right side of the road; park here (N45 34.530' / W122 07.998'). If you get to Wahkeena Falls, you went too far.

From the parking pullout, try to spot the old Multnomah Lodge drain cap that still sits inconspicuously along the side of the Historic Columbia River Highway. After inspecting that little piece of history, start making your way up the obvious path. The trail briefly ascends before meeting up with Mist Creek. Cross here and walk about 30 feet to the site of the old Multnomah Lodge. Keep a sharp eye, as nature is rapidly reclaiming the only evidence of the lodge's existence. Now covered in moss, the stone fireplace has managed to withstand the fire, elements, and curious visitors for over eighty years. The chimney is more than likely unstable though, so please stay off of the structure and take only photographs.

Walk back and cross the creek once more. What exists of a trail is on the west side of Mist Creek. From here the unmaintained boot path turns sharply uphill. Staying near the creek, the trail switches back and forth a few times before encountering a large scree slope. Once the slope has been conquered, the trail pinches its way between a large boulder and the creek before one final ascent to the base of the falls.

Mist Falls

D. Mosier Creek Falls

One of the few easy-to-get-to falls east of the Cascades, Mosier Creek Falls is a quick out-and-back that totals barely half a mile. In that stretch, however, you'll visit a pioneer cemetery, wildflower meadows, a scenic canyon, and a waterfall with a swimmable pool.

To visit Mosier Creek Falls from Hood River, take I-84 east to exit 69. Turn right onto US 30 east and drive through the small town of Mosier. Just after crossing Mosier Creek on a bridge, pull off to the side of the road and park (N45 41.087' / W121 23.638'). At a bench the trail ascends a hillside, skirts a cemetery, and a short time later arrives at 80-foot Mosier Creek Falls.

E. Wah Gwin Gwin Falls

Located on the grounds of the Columbia Gorge Hotel, Phelps Creek plunges over 200 feet into the Columbia River.

To visit the falls, take I-84 to exit 62. The Columbia Gorge Hotel is on the north side of the freeway. Park (N45 42.686' / W121 33.268') and walk through the garden on the east side of the hotel to overlooks atop the falls.

BASALT

Oregon has a rich volcanic history. Most of the waterfalls you'll encounter here are a direct result of some serious volcanic activity. It's hard to imagine that the ledges and outcroppings that waterfalls dance around and plunge over were once lava flows, but that is often the case. Once lava cools it forms the basalt rock that is so common in this area. The two most prevalent types of basalt you'll encounter are entablature and columnar.

Entablature basalt is a relatively fast-cooling lava that often fractures into irregular patterns and joints.

Columnar basalt, meanwhile, forms underneath entablature basalt when lava cools and fractures to form five- or six-sided honeycomb-like pillars.

Over time, the elements, mostly water, have eroded away or scoured out segments of entablature basalt, revealing the columnar basalt underneath. The combination of both makes for a visually stunning accent to a waterfall. Latourell Falls and Abiqua Falls are fine examples. And the hike to Fall Creek Falls walks you through a remarkable canyon where columnar basalt juts out in every direction.

The Coast Range

Camping and Accommodations

Below the Falls Lodge: As fine a stay as can be had at a cabin in the woods. The Below the Falls Lodge sits on Glen Creek just a mile away from Golden and Silver Falls State Park. The private lodge is eco-friendly, cozy, and expertly furnished. The forest views are hauntingly beautiful, and the residence has its own sauna near the creek. (541) 404-9349; belowthefallslodge.com

Best Western Plus Pier Point Inn: Nestled right on the Siuslaw River across from historic Downtown Florence, the Pier Point Inn offers great views and a prime location. 85625 US 101, Florence, OR 97439; (800) 435-6736; bwpierpointinn.com

Inn at Cape Kiwanda: Located across the road from the imposing, albeit lesser-known Haystack Rock, the inn affords breathtaking views. It's also about 100 feet from the renowned Pelican Brewery. 33105 Cape Kiwanda Dr., Pacific City, OR 97135; (888) 965-7001; www.yourlittlebeachtown.com/inn

Liberty Inn: Comfortable, clean, and quiet. The Liberty Inn also serves up a deluxe continental breakfast complete with eggs, sausage, biscuits, and gravy. 4990 NE Logan Rd., Lincoln City, OR 97367; (541) 994-1777; libertyinn.com

The Mill Casino: The Mill offers a number of dining and entertainment options suitable for all budgets and tastes, as well as waterfront views of Coos Bay. 3201 Tremont St., North Bend, OR 97459; (800) 953-4800; themillcasino.com

Overleaf Lodge & Spa: The Overleaf sits on an incredibly scenic chunk of beach in Yachats. Every room has an ocean view, and the entire facility is adorned with impressive and eclectic local art. 2055 US 101, Yachats, OR 97498; (541) 547-4880; overleaflodge.com

Surftides: The smartly renovated Surftides in Lincoln City is located right on the beach. It has a fantastic restaurant and bar, indoor pool, workout room, and fire pits. 2945 NW Jetty Ave., Lincoln City, OR 97367; (541) 994-2191; surftideslincolncity.com

Alsea Falls Recreation Site: Sixteen sites, $12 to $20. (503) 375-5646

Devil's Lake State Recreation Area: More than eighty-five sites, $6 to $40. (541) 994-2002

13 University Falls

While the hike isn't long and the forest is relatively new, the quick jaunt to University Falls is a worthy cause in high-water season.

Height: 55 feet
Distance: 0.8 mile out and back
Elevation gain: 200 feet
Difficulty: Easy
Trail surface: Hard-packed dirt, rocky
Hiking time: About 30 minutes to 1 hour
County: Tillamook

Land status: State forest
Fees and permits: None
Trail contact: Oregon Department of Forestry, Tillamook State Forest, (503) 945-7200, www .oregon.gov/ODF/tillamookstateforest
Map: *DeLorme Atlas & Gazetteer Oregon,* page 21, E8–F8

Finding the trailhead: From Portland, head west on US 26 for 20 miles and take a slight left onto OR 6. Drive for 18.8 miles. Following signs for University Falls, make a left onto Saddle Mountain Road. The road soon approaches a T junction. Make a right here and follow signs to University Falls for 3.5 miles. Look for a small pullout and the trailhead on the right. GPS: N45 35.907' / W123 23.561'

The Hike

From the trailhead the path begins by climbing briefly into the forest. This area has been repeatedly decimated by wildfires, and the forest that does exist here is largely deciduous, with red alder dominating the landscape.

Stay straight at a couple of off-road-vehicle path crossings and begin a slow, easy descent of about 0.2 mile to a junction. Follow the signed path on the left for 0.1 mile to the base of University Falls. There's not much here in the way of picnic areas, but there are a few serviceable rocks. Head back the way you came to complete the hike.

Miles and Directions

0.0 From the trailhead, hike 0.3 mile to a junction, staying straight at a pair of dirt road crossings.

0.3 Take the signed trail on the left that leads to the base of University Falls.

0.4 Arrive at University Falls. Head back the way you came.

0.8 Arrive back at the trailhead.

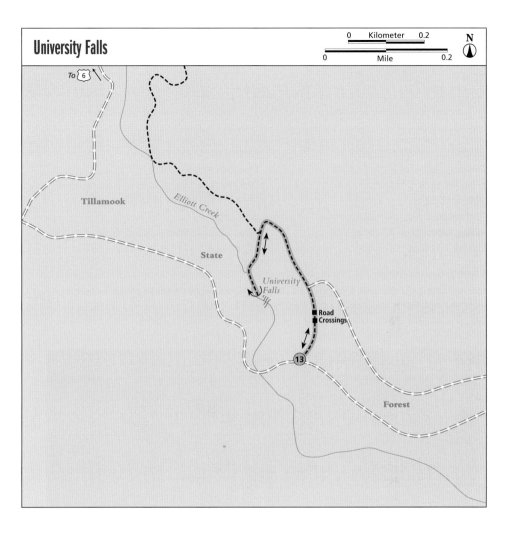

University Falls

To 6

Tillamook

Elliott Creek

State

University Falls

Road
Crossings

13

Forest

0   Kilometer   0.2

0   Mile   0.2

N

14 Munson Creek Falls

At just half a mile, the walk to Munson Creek Falls might not qualify as an actual hike. But if ever there was a leg-stretch of less than a mile worth taking, this is it.

Height: 319 feet (combined drops)
Distance: 0.5 mile out and back
Elevation gain: 110 feet
Difficulty: Easy
Trail surface: Hard-packed dirt, rocky
Hiking time: About 30 minutes
County: Tillamook

Land status: State park
Fees and permits: None
Trail contact: Oregon Parks and Recreation Department, (503) 986-0707, oregonstate parks.org
Map: *DeLorme Atlas & Gazetteer Oregon,* page 26, B4

Finding the trailhead: From Tillamook, drive south on US 101 for 8 miles and turn left at a sign for Munson Falls Natural Site. Drive 1.6 miles to a small turnaround and the trailhead for Munson Creek Falls. GPS: N45 21.937' / W123 46.412'

Munson Creek Falls

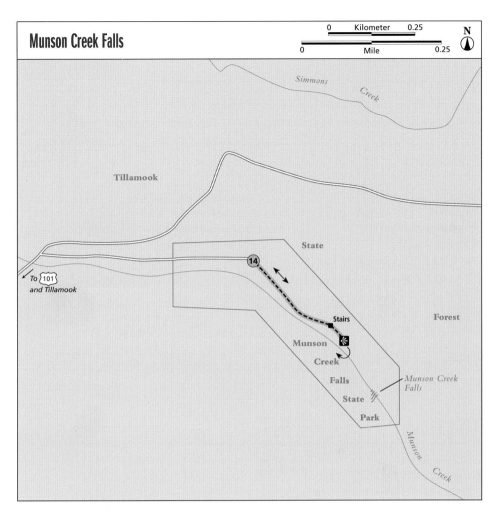

The Hike

From the trailhead, the short stroll to Munson Creek Falls is set among massive old-growth western red cedars and Sitka spruce that drip with moss and lichen. The falls are 319 feet of three-tiered, awe-inspiring, cascade goodness. They are the tallest in the Coast Range and perhaps the tallest in the state west of the Willamette River.

Miles and Directions

0.0 From the trailhead, walk 0.25 mile until the trail peters out at a falls-viewing area.

0.3 Arrive at Munson Creek Falls viewing area (N45 21.824' / W123 46.219'). Head back the way you came.

0.5 Arrive back at the trailhead.

15 Harts Cove/Chitwood Creek Falls

While the chance to see a waterfall that cascades into the ocean is bait enough to get you to Harts Cove, the hike itself is a real winner. Between the waterfall, the old-growth Sitkas, and the sweeping ocean views, you might be hard-pressed to sequence this hike's best attributes. Note that the gated road to the trailhead is closed January 1 through July 15.

Height: 80 feet
Distance: 5.5 miles out and back
Elevation gain: 1,300 feet
Difficulty: Moderate
Trail surface: Hard-packed dirt, rocky
Hiking time: About 2-4 hours
County: Tillamook

Land status: National forest
Fees and permits: None
Trail contact: Hebo Ranger District, (503) 392-5100, www.fs.usda.gov/main/siuslaw/home
Map: *DeLorme Atlas & Gazetteer Oregon*, page 26, F2

Finding the trailhead: Please note that the access road to the trailhead is closed from January 1 through July 15. From Lincoln City, drive north on US 101 to a junction with OR 18. Continue on US 101 for 3.8 miles past this junction. As the road nears a crest, make a left onto unsigned gravel FR 1861. Drive 4 more miles to the end of the road and the trailhead for Harts Cove. GPS: N45 03.898' / W123 59.732'

The Hike

The hike to Harts Cove begins with something almost no hiker wants to encounter at the beginning of a trek: lots of descent. As a matter of fact, you'll be losing close to 600 feet of elevation in the first 0.75 mile, which of course means you'll have your work cut out for you at the end of the hike. But for now, down you go.

After about a half dozen switchbacks through young forest, the trail arrives at a footbridge and the descending is done . . . for now. After the bridge the forest begins to take on a distinctly different feel as old growth works into the mix. After another 0.75 mile of hiking, you get the first view of the end goal. A viewpoint here, complete with a bench, looks down and across a cove toward the meadow you'll be standing in shortly.

Continue 0.4 mile to a creek crossing. There used to be a footbridge at this creek as well, but the last high-water season washed it out. Not to worry, however. The creek is typically in the low-flow category in summer. Cross the creek and continue another easy 0.6 mile. At this point the trail emerges from the forest into a large, open meadow with an ocean view. From here the official path, if there is one, can be tough to discern. But essentially, follow the most well-worn path, which leads steeply down to a group of trees on the other end of the meadow. Be careful here and watch your

Chitwood Creek Falls

footing. There are a couple of nice viewpoints in among the trees that look back toward the creek you crossed minutes earlier, which now tumbles over a cliff as Chitwood Falls. Enjoy lunch with a view, then head back the way you came.

The trails located within Cascade Head Preserve near Lincoln City provide some of the best coastal hiking in the state. The trek out to Harts Cove is just one of a handful of options you'll want to explore while you're in the area.

Miles and Directions

0.0 From the trailhead, hike 0.8 mile down a steep set of switchbacks before arriving at a bridged creek crossing.

0.8 Hike another 0.75 mile and arrive at a viewpoint where the trail turns away from the ocean and heads back toward a ravine.

1.5 Arrive at viewpoint. Continue 0.4 mile to a bridgeless crossing of Chitwood Creek.

1.9 Hike another 0.6 mile to an open meadow.

2.5 Continue 0.25 mile through the meadow to a group of trees and views of Chitwood Falls (N45 04.577' / W124 00.596').

2.8 Arrive at a falls viewpoint. Head back the way you came.

5.6 Arrive back at the trailhead.

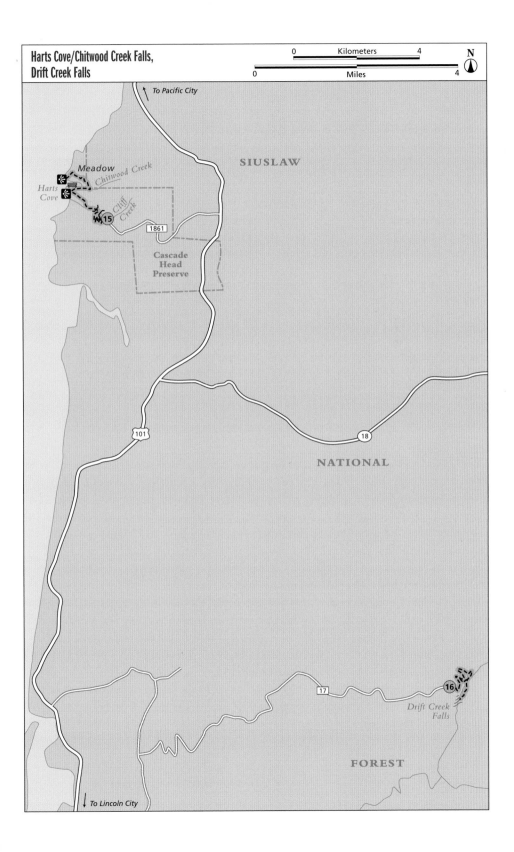

Kilometers

0   4

0   Miles   4

N

To Pacific City

SIUSLAW

Meadow

Chitwood Creek

Harts
Cove

Cliff
Creek

15

1861

Cascade
Head
Preserve

101

18

NATIONAL

17

16

Drift Creek
Falls

FOREST

To Lincoln City

16 Drift Creek Falls

Drift Creek Falls is a 66-foot cascade that is the main attraction of this out-and-back or semi-loop hike. But there's more to this trek than just another pretty waterfall. The first part of the hike is in pleasant second-growth forest, but once you cross a creek bridge, the path leads through some very lush old growth. Then you get to the really exciting stuff.

See map on page 63.
Height: 66 feet
Distance: 3.0 miles out and back or 3.7-mile semi-loop
Elevation gain: 350 feet or 650 feet
Difficulty: Easy to moderate
Trail surface: Hard-packed dirt, rocky
Hiking time: About 1.5–3 hours

County: Lincoln
Land status: National forest
Fees and permits: Northwest Forest Pass or small day-use fee required
Trail contact: Hebo Ranger District, (503) 392-5100, http://fs.usda.gov/siuslaw
Map: DeLorme Atlas & Gazetteer Oregon, page 32, B3

Finding the trailhead: From Portland, take OR 18 toward the coast. Just after milepost 5 (5 miles from US 101), turn left onto Bear Creek Road and drive 9 miles to the trailhead. The road turns into FR 17 along the way, and any questionable junctions are signed. Parking requires a small fee or Northwest Forest Pass. GPS: N44 56.128' / W123 51.333'

The Hike

From the trailhead the path descends and winds its way in and out of ravines through a second-growth forest exploding with sword ferns. After 0.7 mile you'll reach a junction. To do the loop, follow the trail to the left as it ascends into a scenic forest before rejoining the main trail. To do the out-and-back, stay to the right, eventually reaching a footbridge crossing Drift Creek. Now the character of the hike changes as the path explores groves of old-growth Doug fir and western red cedar. After 0.3 mile the trail reaches a 240-foot suspension bridge.

The bridge is where you get your first glimpse of the new-look waterfall. Today, Drift Creek Falls looks considerably different than it had for the past few thousand years. Sometime in August 2010, the face of the basalt wall that the falls tumble over crumbled and fell away in a massive rockslide. The once tranquil pool at the bottom of the waterfall is now a garden of house-size boulders and mini-waterfalls.

Cross the bridge and follow the path the final 0.2 mile down to the base of the falls. Return the way you came. To complete the semi-loop, stay left at the junction after the small footbridge.

Top: Drift Creek Falls
Bottom: Drift Creek Falls from near the base ▶

Drift Creek Falls is one of the best spots in the area to take in the ever-changing Northwest; whether that change is caused by man or by force of nature. From logging to erosion and even human engineering, the hike to Drift Creek Falls puts change on literal and explorable display.

Miles and Directions

0.0   Begin hiking from trailhead on the east end of the parking area.

0.7   Arrive at a junction with the North Loop. Take a left.

1.7   Arrive at a junction. Go left, toward the falls.

2.0   Arrive at the Drift Creek suspension bridge. Continue across the bridge and descend to the lower viewing area of Drift Creek Falls (N44 55.974' / W123 51.067').

2.2   Arrive at the lower falls. Head back the way you came.

2.7   Arrive at junction. Go left to complete the semi-loop.

3.7   Arrive back at the trailhead.

17 Green Peak Falls/Alsea Falls

The Alsea Falls Recreation Site is a popular summer hangout. The long, sliding Alsea Falls is predictably full in spring but low and explorable in warmer weather. Meanwhile, the hike to Green Peak Falls can be confusing, but the forest along the way and the falls at the end are worth it.

Height: Alsea Falls, 30 feet; Green Peak Falls, 45 feet
Distance: 2.5 miles out and back
Elevation gain: 530 feet
Difficulty: Easy
Trail surface: Hard-packed dirt, rocky, gravel
Hiking time: About 1-2 hours
County: Benton

Land status: State forest
Fees and permits: None
Trail contact: Salem district BLM, (503) 375-5646, http://www.blm.gov/or/resources/recreation/site_info.php?siteid=220
Map: DeLorme Atlas & Gazetteer Oregon, page 39, B7

Finding the trailhead: From Corvallis, take OR 34 west for 17 miles and make a left onto South First Street (Alsea-Deadwood Highway). Drive 1 mile and make a left onto South Fork Road. Drive 8 more miles, the last two of which are gravel, to the Alsea Falls Recreation Site on the left. Park near the day-use picnic area. GPS: N44 19.556' / W123 29.466'

The Hike

From the far end of the picnic area, follow a gravel path downstream for about 100 yards to the top of Alsea Falls. Continue down a dirt path that makes its way to the area beneath the falls. Head back up the main parking area and make a left at a footbridge crossing the river.

After crossing the bridge, make a left at a junction and continue hiking. After 0.2 mile you'll come to a junction that offers water access down to the left. Stay straight here and continue hiking through very scenic forest. After another 0.3 mile the trail will bend to the right and join up with a gravel road leading left. Continue along the gravel road, ignoring paths leading down to McBee Park on the left. Once the road descends, look for a signed junction on the right that leads through an open camping area. The trail then reenters the forest and the path continues another 0.4 mile to Green Peak Falls. The area surrounding the falls is good for swimming and exploring. When you've had your fill, return the way you came.

Miles and Directions

0.0 From the far end of the picnic area, follow a gravel path downstream for about 100 yards to Alsea Falls (N44 19.576' / W123 29.510'). Backtrack and cross a footbridge over the river and make a left.

Alsea Falls

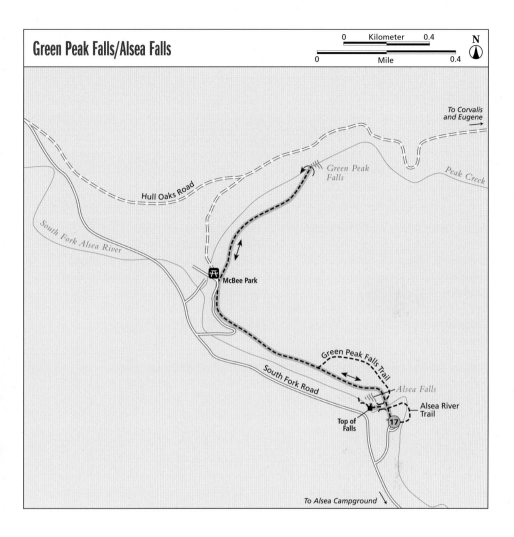

0   Kilometer   0.4

0   Mile   0.4

N

To Corvalis
and Eugene

Green Peak
Falls

Peak Creek

Hull Oaks Road

South Fork Alsea River

McBee Park

Green Peak Falls Trail

South Fork Road

Alsea Falls

Alsea River
Trail

Top of
Falls

17

To Alsea Campground

0.6   The trail bends around to the right and meets up with a gravel road leading to the left. Continue hiking another 0.2 mile to a signed junction on the right that leads through an open camping area. The trail resumes and continues another 0.4 mile to Green Peak Falls (N44 20.133' / W123 29.712').

1.2   Arrive at Green Peak Falls. Head back the way you came.

2.4   Arrive back at the trailhead.

18 Sweet Creek Falls

The hike along Sweet Creek is an absolute joy. There are no thundering cascades or dramatic, vista-laden viewpoints to be found along this trail. There really isn't even all that much exercise to speak of. Instead what you get is a peaceful walk through old-growth forest alongside a stunningly beautiful creek. The trail itself is also remark-able. During the course of this outing, you will walk through a narrow gorge along catwalks bolted to canyon walls, ease through a lush forest, and ascend to a delightful viewpoint of Sweet Creek Falls.

Height: Sweet Creek Falls, 70 feet (combined drops); Annice Falls, 35 feet
Distance: 2.4 miles out and back
Elevation gain: 350 feet
Difficulty: Easy
Trail surface: Hard-packed dirt, metal catwalk
Hiking time: About 1-2 hours
County: Lane

Land status: National forest
Fees and permits: None
Trail contact: Central Coast Ranger District (Florence), (541) 902-8526, www.fs.usda.gov/siuslaw
Map: *DeLorme Atlas & Gazetteer Oregon,* page 45, A8

Finding the trailhead: From Eugene, take OR 126 west for 46 miles. Just before a bridge crossing into the town of Mapleton, make a left onto Sweet Creek Road and drive 10 miles to the Homestead Trailhead parking area on the right. GPS: N43 57.468' / W123 54.123'

The Hike

There are a number of small drops and mini-cascades along the trail here. Though there is some small debate over the exact number of legitimate and named falls, there are at least two: the namesake Sweet Creek Falls and Annice Falls. However many there might actually be and what their official or unofficial names are, this is a leg stretch worth taking.

Miles and Directions

0.0 From the trailhead, follow the path upstream next to Sweet Creek, walking past sev-eral small cascades and a series of massive bigleaf maples and Douglas firs. The trail becomes a set of catwalks through a canyon before reemerging into a lush forest.

0.4 Arrive at the signed Annice Falls (N43 57.241' / W123 54.209').

0.7 Arrive at a junction with a trail that climbs to the Sweet Creek Trailhead. Continue along the main path.

Top: Sweet Creek Falls ▶
Bottom: A catwalk trail segment along Sweet Creek

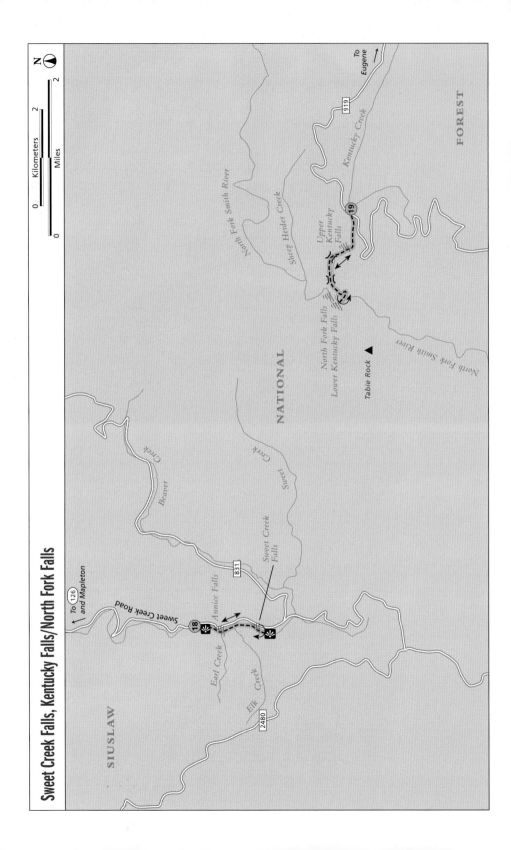

Sweet Creek Falls, Kentucky Falls/North Fork Falls

SIUSLAW

To (126)
and Mapleton

Sweet Creek Road

Earl Creek

831

18

Annice Falls

Braver Creek

Sweet Creek

Sweet Creek Falls

Elk Creek

2480

NATIONAL

North Fork Falls
Lower Kentucky Falls

Table Rock ▲

North Fork Smith River

Sheep Herder Creek

Upper Kentucky Falls

Kentucky Creek

919

To Eugene

FOREST

N

Kilometers
0   2

Miles
0   2

Sweet Creek in autumn

1.1 Arrive at the base of Sweet Creek Falls (N43 56.798' / W123 54.191'). Proceed up the short but steep spur trail leading to an up-close-and-personal view of the falls.

1.2 Arrive at the upper viewpoint (N43 56.760' / W123 54.209'). Head back the way you came.

2.4 Arrive back at the trailhead.

Lower Kentucky Falls

19 Kentucky Falls/North Fork Falls

Some back roads are a joy to drive. Others can be the bane of a waterfall lover's existence. They are often infested with potholes, littered with debris, and play host to the occasional logging truck operating on the very brink of control. But they also aid in our quest for the most remote and scenic places in the Northwest. The hike that leads to Upper Kentucky, Lower Kentucky, and North Fork Falls requires miles of sketchy paved and gravel road driving. But the hike and the falls are scenic enough to install a smile on your face for the entire drive back to civilization.

See map on page 72.
Height: Upper Kentucky Falls, 100 feet; Lower Kentucky Falls, 90 feet; North Fork Falls, 120 feet
Distance: 4.4 miles out and back
Elevation gain: 800 feet
Difficulty: Moderate
Trail surface: Hard-packed dirt, rocky
Hiking time: About 1.5–3 hours

County: Douglas
Land status: National forest
Fees and permits: None
Trail contact: Central Coast Ranger District (Florence), (541) 902-8526, www.fs.usda.gov/siuslaw
Map: *DeLorme Atlas & Gazetteer Oregon,* page 45, A9

Finding the trailhead: From Eugene, take OR 126 west for 33 miles and make a left at a sign for the Whittaker Creek Recreation Area. Drive 1.6 miles and make a right, crossing a bridge. Drive another 1.5 miles and veer left onto Dunn Ridge Road. Continue 7 miles to a junction and make a left onto unpaved Knowles Creek Road. Drive 2.6 more miles and make a right onto FR 23. Turn right on paved FR 919 and drive the final 2.7 miles to the parking area on the right. GPS: N43 55.715' / W123 47.607'

The Hike

The trail begins across the road from the parking area and begins a slow, steady descent through attractive old growth. After 0.6 mile the trail reaches the top of Upper Kentucky Falls and follows a steep set of switchbacks to its base. There are a handful of good angles from which to photograph the falls, but the best are at the bottom.

From here the trail continues an easy amble of 1 mile to a set of descending switchbacks. When the switchbacks end at a junction, stay right and walk around the corner to a viewing platform of North Fork Falls on the left and Lower Kentucky Falls on the right. There's some scrambling and rock hopping to be done here if you'd like a better look at North Fork Falls, and you might as well. It's possible to get a shot of both cascades in the same frame if you can get out there far enough. Return the way you came.

Section of trail on the way to Upper Kentucky Falls

Miles and Directions

0.0 From the trailhead, hike 0.7 mile to the base of Upper Kentucky Falls (N43 55.759' / W123 48.218').

0.6 Continue hiking for 1.3 miles to a junction at the base of a set of switchbacks.

2.1 Arrive at a junction and make a right.

2.2 Arrive at the viewing platform for North Fork Falls (N43 55.845' / W123 49.053') and Lower Kentucky Falls (N43 55.854' / W123 49.038'). Head back the way you came.

4.4 Arrive back at the trailhead.

20 Golden and Silver Falls

The combination of two distinctive waterfalls and a one-of-a-kind historic trail makes the trek to Golden and Silver Falls a destination hike in the Coast Range.

Height: Golden Falls, 200 feet; Silver Falls, 130 feet
Distance: 3.0 miles out and back
Elevation gain: 600 feet
Difficulty: Easy to moderate
Trail surface: Hard-packed dirt, rocky
Hiking time: 1-2 hours
County: Coos

Land status: State natural area
Fees and permits: None
Trail contact: Oregon Parks and Recreation Department: State Parks, (503) 986-0707, oregonstateparks.org
Map: *DeLorme Atlas & Gazetteer Oregon,* page 45, F7

Finding the trailhead: From Coos Bay, follow US 101 south to the signed turn for Eastside or Alleghany. Turn left here and follow the Coos River Highway for 23 miles to the end of the road, following signs for the town of Alleghany, then for the state park. The Silver Falls Trailhead is on the left side of the parking area. GPS: N43 28.969' / W123 55.947'

The Hike

It's recommended that you hike all of the trails in the park because each one offers its own view. But if time is an issue, or you're just not up to all 3 miles of trail, the optimal route starts from the north end of the parking area and crosses a small footbridge before forking. For a view of Golden Falls from the bottom, go right, but for now take a left here, heading toward Silver Falls. The trail parallels the creek through a forest of old-growth Douglas fir and bigleaf maple trees. After 0.4 mile the trail reaches a junction. Continue straight, to the base of Silver Falls. The 130-foot Silver Falls spills over a rounded dome of bedrock in mesmerizing strands of water that dance through midair to the rocks below. Continue the short distance back to the junction and begin the steady climb up to the top of Golden Falls.

The trail that leads to the top of Golden Falls was once a harrowing road that connected a settlement above the cascade with the valley below. What was surely at one point a white-knuckle journey via automobile now affords luxury box views of the falls as well as an encompassing perspective of the drainage that the creek carves. There is a lot of exposure in this area, so proceed with caution. The trail officially ends at the top of the falls, but adventurous types can follow a boot path upstream for quite a ways.

Head back down the trail to the original junction near the footbridge and take the short stroll through an impressive grove of myrtlewood trees to the base of Golden Falls before returning to the parking area. The last section of trail to explore leaves from the other end of the parking area and travels a short 0.3 mile to an excellent, front-side view of Silver Falls. Head back the way you came to complete the hike.

Golden Falls

Silver Falls

The old roadbed turned trail leading to the top of Golden Falls

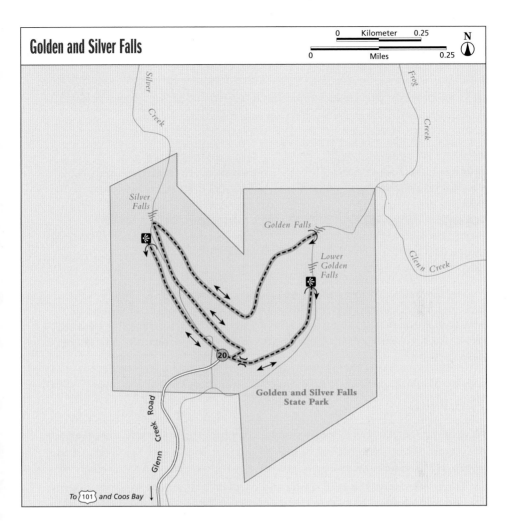

Miles and Directions

0.0 From the parking area, cross a small footbridge and make a left at the junction.

0.4 Continue past a junction to the base of Silver Falls (N43 29.161' / W123 56.101'). Backtrack and make a left at the junction, heading up.

0.9 Arrive at the top of Golden Falls (N43 29.141' / W123 55.712'). Head back to the original junction at the footbridge.

1.8 Make a left and head to the base of Golden Falls (N43 29.059' / W123 55.744').

2.2 Arrive at the base of Golden Falls. Head back the way you came.

2.6 Arrive back at the main parking area. Go to the other end of the parking area and start the hike to the Silver Falls viewpoint.

2.8 Arrive at Silver Falls (N43 29.130' / W123 56.099'). Head back the way you came.

3.0 Arrive at the trailhead.

21 Coquille River Falls

It's a long drive to get to Coquille River Falls no matter how you slice it. With that said, this is one of the premier waterfalls in Oregon's Southern Coast Range and shouldn't be missed by any self-respecting waterfall lover.

Height: 110 feet (combined drops)
Distance: 1.0 mile out and back
Elevation gain: 400 feet
Difficulty: Easy
Trail surface: Hard-packed dirt, rocky
Hiking time: About 30 minutes to 1 hour
County: Coos
Land status: National forest

Fees and permits: None
Trail contact: Powers Ranger District, (541) 439-6200, http://www.fs.usda .gov/recarea/rogue-siskiyou/null/ recarea/?recid=69434&actid=62
Map: *DeLorme Atlas & Gazetteer Oregon,* page 59, C6

Finding the trailhead: From Coos Bay, take I-5 south for 5 miles to OR 42. Take OR 42 for 22.8 miles, passing through the town of Myrtle Point, to a junction with OR 542. Continue 35 miles, passing through the town of Powers. Along the way the road changes to NF-33. Make a left onto NF-3348 and drive the final 1.6 miles to the signed pullout on the left. GPS: N42 42.801' / W124 01.393'

The Hike

From the pullout, the trail descends steeply, switchbacking for 0.5 mile to a viewpoint of Coquille River Falls. After all of that driving, a half mile isn't that much of a leg stretch, so take your time.

The falls are thunderous in spring and maintain a lower but still very attractive flow through summer. The upper tier drops 45 feet before splitting off into two segments and plunging a final 65 feet. Near the base, Drowned-Out Creek enters the Coquille River and offers its own series of mini-cascades. It's possible to scramble down to the base of the falls, but exercise caution as it can be slick in spots.

Miles and Directions

0.0 From the pullout, follow the trail 0.5 mile to a viewpoint of Coquille River Falls (N42.71782' / W124.02073').

0.5 Arrive at a viewpoint of the falls. Head back the way you came.

1.0 Arrive back at the trailhead.

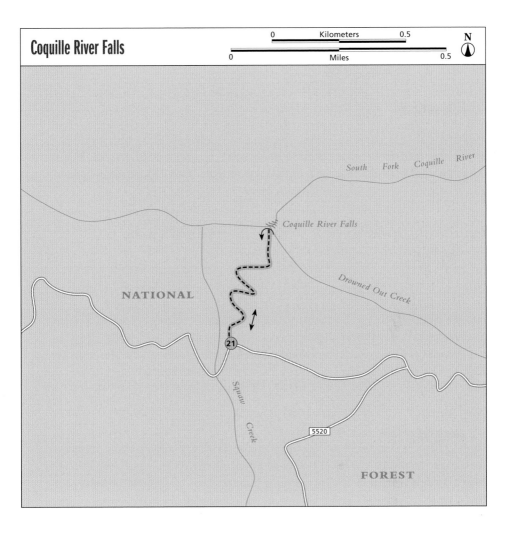

Honorable Mentions

F. Fishhawk Falls

Fishhawk Falls is a beautiful, veiling cascade that tumbles 72 feet over two drops. It rests within the Lee Wooden County Park, which is nice enough on its own. But just down the road from the falls, the Jewell Meadows State Wildlife Management Area is also worth a visit if you happen to be in the area.

To visit the falls from Astoria, take OR 202 south for 23 miles. The Lee Wooden County Park and Fishhawk Falls will be on the right (N45 57.500' / W123 35.017').

G. Hug Point

At 15 feet, Hug Point Falls is hardly a thundering cascade, but it sure is pretty! A favorite among photographers, Hug Point Falls drops directly onto the beach and into the ocean. It's best to try to access the falls when tides are low because you have to walk around a headland to access the falls.

To visit the falls from Cannon Beach, drive south on US 101 for 4.2 miles and then make a right into Hug Point State Park. From the parking area, head down the stairs and walk to the right, around the headland and to the falls (N45 49.800' / W123 57.716').

H. Youngs River Falls

A member of the Lewis and Clark expedition discovered Youngs River Falls. On March 1, 1806, Patrick Gass was leading a hunting party and noted the falls for the first time by a European. The 54-foot falls are substantial and make a great place to spend an afternoon.

To visit the falls from Astoria, take Youngs River Road south for 7.3 miles and turn right at the signed parking area (N46 04.089' / W123 47.302') for Youngs River Falls. A short trail leads to the water and good views of the falls.

I. Elk Creek Falls

Elk Creek Falls used to be a no-brainer. It was just off the side of the road on the way to Coquille River Falls. Dropping 130 feet over two drops, it is a very photogenic cascade. Unfortunately a landslide closed the road to Coquille River Falls, but the trip out to see the Elk Creek Cascade is still a worthy endeavor for waterfall lovers.

To visit the falls from Coos Bay, follow US 101 south to OR 42. Follow OR 42 south for about 21 miles and turn right onto the Rogue-Coquille Scenic Byway. Follow this road, which becomes FR 33, for about 17.6 miles to the signed pullout on the left (N42 48.993' / W124 00.778'). The falls are about 200 yards up the trail.

Elk Creek Falls

MOSSES AND LICHENS

If you're looking to grow things, nutrient-rich rock or soil and a lot of water make a great starter kit. The western side of Oregon's Cascade Range is a prime example of just how well that combination works. Mosses, which are plants, and lichens, which are a mix of fungus and algae, grow profusely in rain-drenched forests. Add an even more constant water source, like a waterfall, and you can get flora that thrives and blooms in an otherworldly array of colors and textures. And while most plants and flowers bloom during the warm-weather months, mosses and lichens are at their peak when it's cold and wet.

Umbrella Falls (Hike 24)

Little Zigzag Falls (Hike 25)

Little Pup Creek Falls (Hike 26)

Northern Oregon Cascades

Camping and Accommodations

Olallie Lake Resort: Cabins, campgrounds, a lake, and a cascade peak. The Olallie Lake Resort offers hiking, fishing, and a stunning view of Mount Jefferson. olallielake resort.com

The Resort at the Mountain: More activities than you can shake a stick at dot the grounds of the Resort at the Mountain, including golf, tennis, croquet, and volleyball. There's also an on-site spa and tons of hiking in every direction. 68010 E. Fairway Ave., Welches, OR 97067; (877) 439-6774; theresort.com

Timberline Lodge: The iconic lodge is equally known for its history, views, and recreational opportunities. Eat, play, and sleep with Mount Hood standing over your shoulder. 27500 W. Leg Rd., Timberline Lodge, OR 97028; (800) 547-1406; timber-linelodge.com

Lost Creek Campground: Sixteen sites, $19 to $35 a night. (503) 668-1700
Roaring River Campground: Fourteen sites, $14 a night. (503) 668-1700
Sherwood Campground: Fourteen sites, $12 a night. (503) 668-1700

22 Ramona Falls

Ramona Falls is one of those natural wonders that must be seen in person. It is vast, and photos do it little justice. The cascade begins narrowly at the top of a large palisade of lava rock. The water quickly spreads across the breadth of the wall before dropping delicately over moss-covered, stair-like columnar basalt. Sun and shadows create rainbows, glowing water, and other visual highlights that vary throughout the day.

Height: 120 feet

Distance: 7.5-mile lollipop-loop hike

Elevation gain: 1,200 feet

Difficulty: Moderate

Trail surface: Hard-packed dirt, sand, rocky

Hiking time: About 2.5–5 hours

County: Clackamas

Land status: Wilderness

Fees and permits: Northwest Forest Pass or small day-use fee required

Trail contact: Zigzag Ranger District, (503) 622-3190

Map: *DeLorme Atlas & Gazetteer Oregon,* page 30, B4

Finding the trailhead: To get there from Portland, travel along US 26 toward Mount Hood for 42 miles. In the town of Zigzag, turn left onto East Lolo Pass Road and drive 4.2 miles. Turn right onto FR 1825 and after 0.7 mile turn right again to cross a bridge. After 1.6 miles, bear left onto FR 100 and travel the final half mile to the road's end and the trailhead. GPS: N45 23.202' / W121 49.909'

Ramona Falls

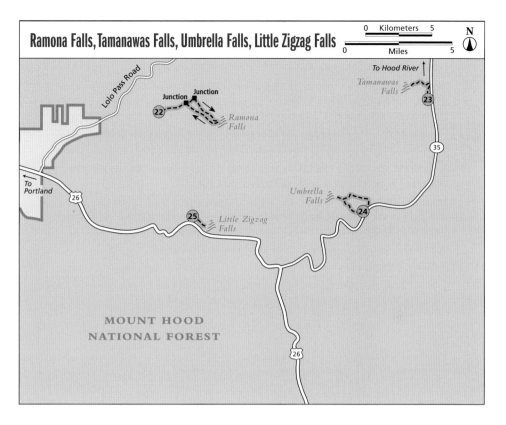

Ramona Falls, Tamanawas Falls, Umbrella Falls, Little Zigzag Falls

Kilometers 5

Miles 5

N

To Hood River

Tamanawas Falls

23

35

Lolo Pass Road

Junction   Junction

22

Ramona Falls

To Portland

26

Umbrella Falls

24

25

Little Zigzag Falls

MOUNT HOOD NATIONAL FOREST

26

The Hike

The hike to Ramona Falls is a scenic stroll that provides a chance to cross the Sandy River while it is little more than a small stream consisting primarily of glacial runoff. After crossing the Sandy, Mount Hood makes a stunning appearance before the hike reenters the trees.

After 1.5 miles of total hiking, you'll come to a junction. Either way will get you to the falls, but this time we'll go left and continue 0.6 mile to another junction. This time turn right and walk through a horse gate. The trail now leads to the shaded beauty of Ramona Creek. This is one of the coolest stretches of the hike. The walk beside Ramona Creek looks and feels more like a forested fantasyland than a hiking trail. After 2 more miles, the trail rounds a corner and delivers you to 120-foot Ramona Falls. If ever there was a place to enjoy a picnic, it is in the large, shaded amphitheater surrounding Ramona Falls.

After lunch, follow the trail up the ridge and out of the trees. Bear right here and follow the trail as it parallels the Sandy for 0.9 mile, returning to the first junction you encountered. Stay straight and hike another 1.5 miles back to the trailhead.

Miles and Directions

0.0 From the trailhead, hike along a wide trail that parallels the Sandy River.

1.2 Arrive at the Sandy River crossing. There is a seasonal bridge here that is usually in place from early spring to sometime in October. The exact location can vary by season, but the trail is usually well worn and flagged on both sides of the Sandy River. Continue hiking on the other side of the river, following either a well-worn trail or flagging upriver to a junction.

1.5 Arrive at a junction. Take the trail to the left and hike 0.5 mile to another junction.

2.1 Arrive at another junction. Turn right here and pass through a horse-stopping gate. Hike 2 more miles along Ramona Creek to the base of the falls.

4.1 Arrive at Ramona Falls (N45 22.802' / W121 46.588'). To complete the loop, continue past the falls and bear right. Turn right again to hike along a horse path that parallels the Sandy River. Follow this trail 1.5 miles down to the first junction you reached. Continue down to the Sandy River crossing and back toward the parking area.

7.5 Arrive back at the trailhead.

23 Tamanawas Falls

As Cold Spring Creek flows away from the eastern side of Mount Hood, it tumbles over a 125-foot cliff to form a thundering wall of water known as Tamanawas Falls.

See map on page 87.
Height: 125 feet
Distance: 3.8 miles out and back
Elevation gain: 700 feet
Difficulty: Easy
Trail surface: Hard-packed dirt, rocky
Hiking time: About 2–3 hours
County: Hood River

Land status: National forest
Fees and permits: Northwest Forest Pass or small day-use fee required
Trail contact: Hood River Ranger District, (541) 352-6002
Map: *DeLorme Atlas & Gazetteer Oregon*, page 30, B5

Finding the trailhead: To get there take I-84 east to Hood River. Head south on OR 35 around Mount Hood to the East Fork Trailhead near milepost 72. Park near the north end of the pullout and walk down toward the creek to pick up the trail. GPS: N45 23.827' / W121 34.307'

The Hike

Known for its stunning color in fall, its formidable icy amphitheater in winter, and its scenic creek, the Tamanawas Falls hike is a solid choice whenever you decide to make the trek. The path to Tamanawas crosses multiple bridges as it ambles its way up through a forested canyon. The clear waters of Cold Spring Creek are a constant and welcome companion for most of the hike.

If you're up for a bit of an adventure, you can tiptoe your way through a mossy talus field to the cave behind the falls; just mind your footing. There is plenty of room to sit and enjoy the view, but don't expect it to be quiet. The ground rumbles and the falls thunder from this vantage.

From the pullout, walk down through the woods toward the sound of the east fork of the Hood River. Then cross a large footbridge and turn right onto the East Fork Trail. After half a mile stay left at the junction with the Cold Springs Trail and cross Cold Spring Creek. Hike another 0.9 mile, stay left at a junction, and continue the final 0.4 mile to the falls. Then head back the way you came.

Miles and Directions

0.0 Hike from the trailhead down to a footbridge crossing, then turn right onto the East Fork Trail.

0.6 Stay left at a junction with the Cold Springs Trail. Continue hiking, staying left at another junction, and proceed the final 0.4 mile to the falls.

1.9 Arrive at Tamanawas Falls. Head back the way you came.

3.8 Arrive back at the trailhead.

Tamanawas Falls

24 Umbrella Falls

The hike to Umbrella Falls is a Northwest summertime classic. Along the trail expect to see beautiful alpine meadows filled with beargrass, lupine, paintbrush, and the occasional tantalizing view of Mount Hood. Umbrella Falls lives up to its name visually and is a great area for picnicking and exploring. The viewpoint of Sahale Falls doesn't offer much but perhaps entices a better view from the old highway.

See map on page 87.
Height: Umbrella Falls, 59 feet; Sahale Falls, 78 feet
Distance: 4.2-mile loop
Elevation gain: 940 feet
Difficulty: Moderate
Trail surface: Hard-packed dirt, rocky
Hiking time: About 2–3 hours

County: Hood River
Land status: National forest
Fees and permits: None
Trail contact: Mount Hood National Forest Headquarters, (503) 668-1700, www.fs.usda .gov/recarea/mthood
Map: *DeLorme Atlas & Gazetteer Oregon,* page 30, C5

Finding the trailhead: From Hood River, drive south on OR 35 for 31 miles. Once passed the marked turnoff for Teacup Lake Sno-Park and Clark Creek Sno-Park, make your next right and drive 0.6 mile to the large Elk Meadows and Sahale Falls trailhead on the right. GPS: N45 19.327' / W121 37.994'

The Hike

From the trailhead, the hike begins with a gentle but steady ascent into fragrant, subalpine woods. After 0.4 mile you'll encounter an intersection with the Umbrella Falls Trail. Make a left here and begin a still steady but steeper ascent that passes beneath chairlifts for Hood River Meadows. The trail also leads through a set of remarkable wildflower meadows, one of which features Mount Hood as a backdrop.

After another 1.4 miles you'll reach a junction. To the left is Sahale Falls. But for now, make a right here, and continue another 0.3 mile to Umbrella Falls. The horsetail-style cascade spreads out and spills gently over multicolored bedrock into a very serviceable swimming hole.

From Umbrella Falls, backtrack to the junction and make a right, heading toward Sahale Falls. Now hike 1.1 miles to a junction with a boot path on the right that leads down to a somewhat precarious viewpoint of the top of Sahale Falls and a bridge that used to be part of the old Mount Hood Highway. The best views of Sahale can be had by scrambling down to the bridge, but most routes are steep, so exercise caution.

Back at the main trail, hike 0.4 mile to a road crossing with another great view of Mount Hood. Pick up the trail on the other side of the road and hike the last 0.1 mile through a potentially swampy bit before ending back at the parking area.

Mt. Hood peeks out on the trail to Umbrella Falls.

Miles and Directions

0.0 From the trailhead, hike 0.4 mile to a junction.

0.4 Arrive at a junction with the Umbrella Falls Trail and make a left.

1.9 Arrive at a junction. Make a right toward Umbrella Falls.

2.2 Arrive at Umbrella Falls. Hike back to the junction and make a right toward Sahale Falls.

3.6 Arrive at a junction with the boot path on the right that leads to a viewpoint of the top of Sahale Falls. Continue down the main trail.

4.1 Arrive at a road crossing. Pick up the trail on the other side. Continue hiking to the parking area.

4.2 Arrive back at the parking area.

25 Little Zigzag Falls

If you blink you'll miss it—but there's a lot to miss. The mini-trek to Little Zigzag Falls is a short but sweet deep forest hike with all the glorious attributes of old growth. A lush canopy and a duffy trail with Little Zigzag River as a constant companion make it a welcome leg stretch or afternoon family hike.

See map on page 87.
Height: 41 feet
Distance: 0.6 mile out and back
Elevation gain: 50 feet
Difficulty: Easy
Trail surface: Hard-packed dirt, rocky, duffy
Hiking time: About 30 minutes
County: Clackamas

Land status: National forest
Fees and permits: Northwest Forest Pass or small day-use fee required May 15 to Oct 1
Trail contact: Mount Hood National Forest Headquarters, (503) 668 1700, www.fs.usda .gov/recarea/mthood
Map: *DeLorme Atlas & Gazetteer Oregon,* page 30, C3

Finding the trailhead: From the town of Rhododendron, drive east on US 26 for 4.3 miles and make a left onto Kiwanis Camp Road. Drive another 2 miles to the road's end and the parking area for Little Zigzag Falls. GPS: N45 18.847' / W121 47.755'

The Hike

At the parking area, it's worth reading the interpretive signs and inspecting some remnants of the old Mount Hood Highway before beginning the hike. When you're ready, make your way over to the signed trailhead and begin.

The trail stays close to the Little Zigzag River, and with good reason. Though it's only 0.3 mile to the falls, there are numerous photogenic spots that might require a few moments' worth of contemplation.

The trail ends at the base Little Zigzag Falls and its major-league-level splash pool and beach area. Being partially spring fed, the cascade maintains a robust presentation all year long. Return the way you came.

Miles and Directions

0.0   From the trailhead, hike 0.3 mile to the falls.
0.3   Arrive at Little Zigzag Falls. Head back the way you came.
0.6   Arrive back at the trailhead.

26 Pup Creek Falls

The Clackamas River is a mecca for outdoors lovers in the greater Portland area. Camping, whitewater rafting, fishing, and, of course, hiking are all popular activities along the length of the Clackamas. One way to get a prime sampling of the river's beauty is by hiking the Clackamas River Trail to Pup Creek Falls.

Height: 237 feet (combined drops)
Distance: 7.8 miles out and back
Elevation gain: 1,100 feet
Difficulty: Moderate to difficult
Trail surface: Gravel, hard-packed dirt, rocky
Hiking time: About 3-5 hours
County: Clackamas
Land status: National forest

Fees and permits: Northwest Forest Pass or small day-use fee required
Trail contact: Clackamas Ranger District, (503) 630-6861 http://www.fs.usda.gov/recarea/mthood/null/recarea/?recid=52774&actid=29
Map: DeLorme Atlas & Gazetteer Oregon, page 29, E10

Finding the trailhead: To get there from Portland, take I-205 to exit 12 and travel 18 miles east to Estacada. Go through town and continue 14.5 miles on OR 224. Just prior to crossing the second of two steel bridges, turn right onto Fish Creek Road. Continue 0.2 mile, cross a bridge, and park at the lot on the right. The trailhead is located at the far end of the parking lot and across the road. GPS: N45 09.416' / W122 09.039'

The Hike

The running waters of the Clackamas River are a fine sight anytime of year. The trail rises and falls as it parallels the waterway, visiting a couple of nice water-access areas and beaches that beg to be explored. These are prime spots for snack breaks and rock skipping. The path also leads to some stunning cliff-edge viewpoints, but be sure to mind younger hikers in these areas. The first 2 miles of the hike passes through the remains of a 2003 forest fire. This area is also teaming with poison oak. The landscape then transitions into an old-growth setting complete with nurse logs and stream crossings complemented by mini-waterfalls.

The visually striking yet little-known Pup Creek Falls makes a great turnaround point. Rich-green mosses and bright-yellow and orange lichens highlight the three-tiered 237-foot falls.

Miles and Directions

0.0 Begin hiking from the trailhead, located at the far end of the parking lot and across the road.

3.6 Arrive at a power-line clearing. There is a somewhat faint boot path on the right side of the trail just before the main trail descends to cross Pup Creek. Sometimes it is marked, sometimes it isn't, so keep a sharp eye. Follow the side trail for 0.3 mile to Pup Creek Falls (GPS: N45 08.808' / W122 06.334'). Head back the way you came.

7.8 Arrive back at the trailhead.

Pup Creek Falls

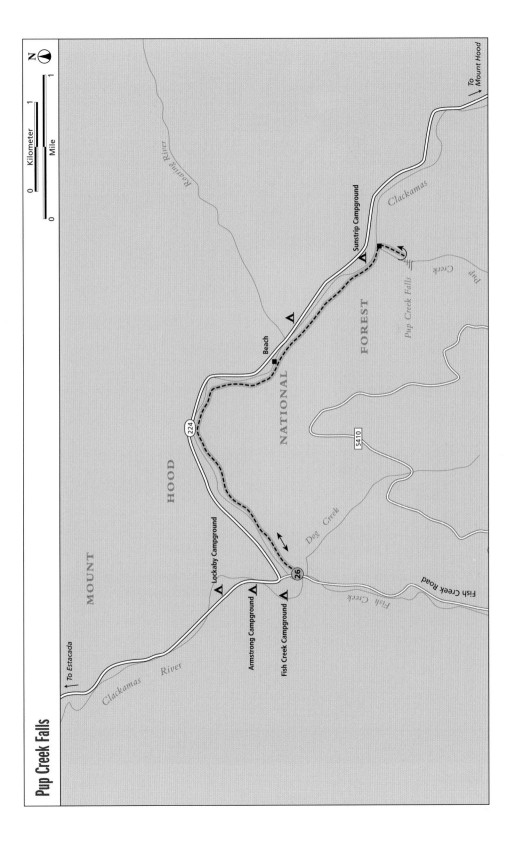

Abiqua Falls

27 Abiqua Falls

Nestled in the hills above the small town of Scotts Mills hides a waterfall lover's dream. Getting to Abiqua Falls is part trek, part hike, and part scramble. The 92-foot falls tumbles into a massive arena of columnar basalt, colored red and green by lichens and moss.

Height: 92 feet
Distance: 1.0 mile out and back
Elevation gain: 350 feet
Difficulty: Moderate
Trail surface: Boot path, creek side
Hiking time: About 1–2 hours
County: Marion

Land status: State forest; falls are on private property
Fees and permits: None
Trail contact: Mount Angel Abbey, (503) 845-3345
Map: *DeLorme Atlas & Gazetteer Oregon,* page 35, A6

Finding the trailhead: From I-205 in Oregon City, take exit 10 and follow OR 213 south for 21 miles. Make a left on South Nowlans Bridge Road for 2.5 miles to the town of Scotts Mills. From there, head south on Crooked Finger Road until it turns to gravel after about 9.4 miles. Turn right on an unmarked gravel road 1.5 miles from the end of pavement. Drive straight through a gated area. Stay straight at any junctions for the next 2.5 miles until the road ends at a locked gate. Park here in the small pullout. GPS: N44 55.858' / W122 34.055'
Please note that the last few miles of driving to Abiqua Falls are rough. It can technically be negotiated in a passenger vehicle, at a very slow rate of speed, however.

The Hike

Beautiful anytime of year and stunning when in full throat, Abiqua Falls is a fantastic off-the-beaten-path destination. Though surrounded by patches of clear-cut above, once down at creek level, the scenery is as good as it gets. Have a camera handy, as there may not be a single unphotogenic angle to shoot.

There is no officially maintained trail to Abiqua Falls. The entire hike is a mere 1 mile out and back. Don't be fooled by the lack of distance, however. Most folks will work up a sweat on the way down, never mind coming back up. The falls themselves are on land owned by the Mount Angel Abbey. The abbey has been gracious enough to allow visitation to the falls thus far, but that can change, so please show ample respect to the land while visiting.

From where you parked, walk back along the road about 60 feet. Take a right onto a small skid road. Follow this down for another 100 or more feet. Just before entering a clear-cut area, there is an obvious boot path heading down into the trees to the left. There are many ambiguous trails in this area. If you find yourself dangerously skirting the ridge above the creek, you've passed the proper trail. If you encounter

Abiqua Falls and Butte Creek Falls

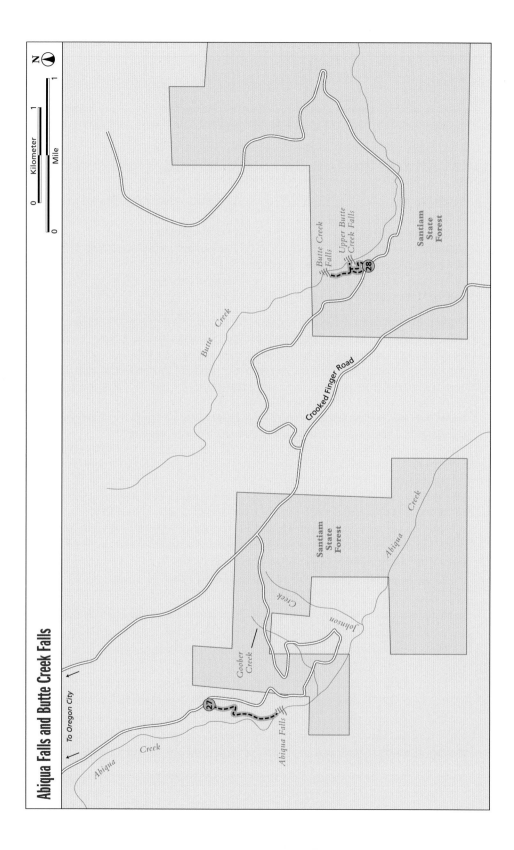

signage from the Abbey Foundation of Oregon, you're on the right track. The signs simply declare that you are entering private property that is available for recreational use only.

The path descends steeply for 0.2 mile to the creek. On my last visit there were ropes that aided in the steeper sections; but these aren't official and should be trusted as much as you would trust any installation of unknown origin. Once you arrive at the water, turn upstream and make your way along the creek bed for another 0.3 mile to the falls. While the path and direction are never in question, there are some tricky areas to negotiate where there are a couple of different routes to choose from. None are wrong.

Depending on the time of year, the falls will probably be heard before seen. The final approach conjures a moment of heightened anticipation, as the falls themselves can't be seen until the moment of arrival.

Miles and Directions

0.0   Begin hiking along the boot path.

0.2   Arrive at the creek. Head upstream.

0.5   Arrive at Abiqua Falls (N44 55.576' / W122 34.066'). Head back the way you came.

1.0   Arrive back at the trailhead.

28 Butte Creek Falls

This hike provides more bang for the buck. Butte Creek and Upper Butte Creek Falls would be fine destinations all by their lonesome. They are both beautiful and one-of-a-kind. But pair the two in the same hike with a truly memorable forest trail and you have as fine an outing as 1 mile can produce.

See map on page 98.
Height: Upper Butte Creek Falls, 26 feet; Butte Creek Falls, 78 feet
Distance: 1.0-mile semi-loop
Elevation gain: 230 feet
Difficulty: Easy
Trail surface: Hard-packed dirt, rocky
Hiking time: About 30 minutes to 1 hour

County: Marion
Land status: State forest
Fees and permits: None
Trail contact: Santiam State Forest, (503) 859-2151
Map: *DeLorme Atlas & Gazetteer Oregon,* page 35, A6

Finding the trailhead: From the town of Scotts Mills, follow Crooked Finger Road for 11.4 miles and turn left onto FR 400. Drive 1.8 more miles to the Butte Creek Falls Trailhead on the left. GPS: N44 55.266' / W122 30.682'

The Hike

From the parking area, begin by taking the leftmost of two potential trails. Follow the path as it descends into the forest and arrives at a junction 0.2 mile later. Take the path leading left toward the lower of the two falls. Continue hiking for another 0.2 mile through lush forest to a rocky outcropping and a viewpoint of Butte Creek Falls.

The Butte Creek Falls viewpoint is a truly memorable one, as it provides 360 degrees of stunning view. After the falls the creek horseshoes through a deep canyon, bending its way around the viewpoint. The falls itself is surrounded by a richly colored, picturesque forest and tumbles into an eye-catching splash pool. The pool is accessible via a steep scramble from the viewpoint, which is doable, but exercise caution.

Continue back to the junction with the trail leading to the upper falls and follow it for 0.1 mile, passing a junction with the return trail before arriving at Upper Butte Creek Falls. This broad, curtain-like cascade is only 26 feet tall but has been undercut by the creek enough to form a very explorable area behind the falls. This falls suffers a bit photogenically in low water conditions, but just like the lower falls, Upper Butte Creek Falls is served well by the surrounding flora. Make your way back up to the junction with the return trail and make a left. The path now climbs gently, looping back to the parking area after 0.2 mile.

Top: Butte Creek Falls
Bottom: Trail in Butte Creek

Miles and Directions

0.0 From the trailhead, hike 0.2 mile to a junction.

0.2 From a signed junction, take the trail to the left leading to the lower falls.

0.4 Arrive at the end off the official trail on a rocky outcropping and a view of Butte Creek Falls (N44 55.460' / W122 30.742'). Hike back the way you came.

0.6 Arrive back at the junction. Stay left toward the upper falls, passing a junction with the return trail.

0.7 Arrive at Upper Butte Creek Falls (N44 55.354' / W122 30.653'). Hike back to the junction with the return trail.

0.8 Arrive at return trail junction. Stay left and hike 0.2 mile to the parking area.

1.0 Arrive back at the trailhead.

Upper Butte Creek Falls

WILDFLOWERS

With varieties and colors almost too numerous to tally, it's understandable that hikers in the Northwest enjoy wildflowers. Here are some favorites you can expect to find alongside the trails in Oregon.

Balsamroot

Indian paintbrush

Trilliums

Larkspur

Calypso orchid

Beargrass

Proxy Falls viewpoint (Hike 37)

Central Oregon Cascades

Camping and Accommodations

Five Pine Lodge and Conference Center: The cabins of the Five Pine Lodge offer up rustic luxury. In addition to the deluxe cabins, the Five Pine campus is home to a spa, a movie theater, and Three Creeks Brewing. 1021 E. Desperado Trail, Sisters, OR 97759; (866) 974-5900; fivepinelodge.com

Lodge at Eagle Crest Resort: The fully renovated lodge offers all the amenities you could hope for, as well as complimentary "adventure planning." Located just north of Bend and within a stone's throw of numerous hikes, the Eagle Crest Lodge also has golf and excellent dining options. 7555 Falcon Crest Dr., Redmond, OR 97756; (855) 682-4786; www.eagle-crest.com/lodging

Seventh Mountain Resort: Settled against the Deschutes River, the Seventh Mountain Resort offers things like golf and whitewater rafting trips in the summer and Nordic skiing and ice skating in the winter. 18575 SW Century Dr., Bend, OR 97702; (877) 765-1501; seventhmountain.com

Tipi Village Retreat: A truly unique lodging experience, the Tipi Village Retreat is hidden away next to a creek in the woods. After a restful sleep in a comfortable tipi, enjoy a gourmet breakfast prepared with farm-fresh eggs from the property. 39615 Wendling Rd., Marcola, OR 97454; (541) 933-1145; www.tipivillageretreat.com/retreat.html

Blue Pool Campground: Twenty-four sites, $16 a night. (541) 225-6300

Cascadia State Park: The tranquil state park is set in a beautiful forest and offers hiking, swimming, fishing, and an off-leash area for dogs. Twenty-five sites, $13 to $17 a night. (541) 367-6021

Elkhorn Valley Recreation Site: Twenty-three sites, $14 a night. (503) 375-5646

McKay Crossing Campground: Sixteen sites, $10 a night. The 23-foot McKay Crossing Falls is located in the campground. (541) 383-5300

Shady Cove Campground: Thirteen sites, $8 a night. (541) 225-6300

Silver Falls State Park: More than eighty sites ranging from tent to cabin, $15 to $39 a night. (503) 873-8681

29 Silver Falls State Park / Trail of Ten Falls

Silver Falls State Park offers a diverse array of services, from primitive campgrounds and cabins to horse corrals and a conference center. But the crown jewel of the park is the Trail of Ten Falls. This loop hike is arguably as spectacular and scenic as any in Oregon.

Height: Winter Falls, 134 feet; Upper North Falls, 65 feet; North Falls, 136 feet; Twin Falls, 31 feet; Double Falls, 184 feet (combined drops); Middle North Falls, 106 feet; Drake Falls, 27 feet; Lower North Falls, 30 feet; Lower South Falls, 93 feet; South Falls, 177 feet
Distance: 5.2- or 8.2-mile loop
Elevation gain: 600 feet or 1,000 feet
Difficulty: Moderate to difficult
Trail surface: Paved, hard-packed dirt, rocky

Hiking time: About 1.5–5 hours
County: Marion
Land status: State park
Fees and permits: There is a $5 day-use fee.
Trail contact: Oregon Parks and Recreation Department, (503) 986-0707, oregonstateparks.org
Map: *DeLorme Atlas & Gazetteer Oregon,* page 34, B5

Finding the trailhead: From downtown Salem, head west on State Street and drive 11.8 miles. Turn right onto Cascade Highway SE and drive 3.6 miles. Turn left onto the Silver Falls Highway and drive 7.8 miles, arriving at Silver Falls State Park. The recommended starting point in this guidebook is from the South Falls parking area. GPS: N44 52.748' / W122 39.401'

The Hike

During this epic outing you'll pass by no fewer than ten waterfalls ranging in height from 27 to 177 feet. The trail occasionally leads behind waterfalls, affording the opportunity to look for tree wells. These round holes in the ceilings of the caverns behind the falls were formed millions of years ago. Occasionally a lava flow would encounter a tree and harden around it while the tree eventually burned away. Water erosion did the rest, moving away soil from underneath the lava rock and leaving behind tree wells.

The waterfalls are the primary draw, but beautiful forest, deep opal pools of water, and striking canyon views rank highly as well. Another asset is the flexibility to choose where to start and how far to hike. There are two main trailheads and a third with a 2-hour time limit to choose from, giving you the option of reducing the hike to a more manageable 5.2-mile loop that still passes most of the larger falls.

I recommend starting at the South Falls parking area and taking the Rim Trail toward Winter Falls. This might seem counterintuitive because it leads you away from

Top: South Falls
Bottom: The trail leading behind Lower South Falls

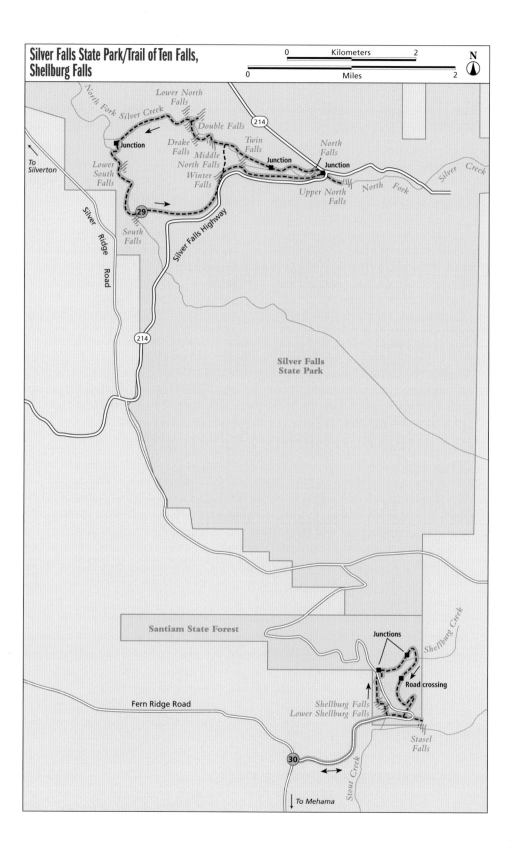

Silver Falls State Park/Trail of Ten Falls, Shellburg Falls

Kilometers
0   2

Miles
0   2

N

North Fork Silver Creek

Lower North Falls

Double Falls

Drake Falls

Middle North Falls

Twin Falls

North Falls

214

Junction

Junction

Junction

To Silverton

Lower South Falls

Winter Falls

Upper North Falls

North Fork

Silver Creek

29

Silver Ridge Road

South Falls

Silver Falls Highway

214

Silver Falls State Park

Santiam State Forest

Junctions

Shellburg Creek

Road crossing

Fern Ridge Road

Shellburg Falls
Lower Shellburg Falls

Stasel Falls

30

Stout Creek

To Mehama

South Falls, the largest waterfall on the trail. It's all a matter of personal preference, but I enjoy the "best for last" approach. If you're taking the shorter loop, turn left onto the Winter Trail when you arrive at the Winter Falls Trailhead, and then left again when you reach a junction with the Canyon Trail.

The path will loop back to South Falls and the South Falls parking area. If you're making the full loop and it's high-water season, it's worth taking the steep path down to the base of Winter Falls for the full view. If it's late summer and you don't feel like hoofing it down to the base and back up, nobody will hold it against you. Continue past Winter Falls on the Rim Trail, making your way up to North Falls.

When you reach the junction at North Falls, take the short 0.2-mile jaunt to the right to visit Upper North Falls, and then return to the massive North Falls. The trail descends down to and behind the thundering North Falls. Continue along the Canyon Trail, visiting the rest of the ten falls along the way. The trail loops back to South Falls and the parking area where you started.

Miles and Directions

0.0 From the South Falls parking area, hike up the Rim Trail toward Winter Falls, away from South Falls.

1.2 Arrive at Winter Falls Trailhead (N44 53.065' / W122 38.434'). Head down to the left for the shorter loop or to view the falls. To complete the shorter loop, make a left at the junction with the Canyon Trail and continue on this path until you arrive back at the parking area. For the longer loop, continue along the Rim Trail.

2.3 Arrive at the junction with North Falls. Take the short trip to the right to visit Upper North Falls (N44 52.979' / W122 36.935') and then return to North Falls (N44 53.119' / W122 37.374'). Take the descending Canyon Trail and continue hiking to Twin Falls (N44 53.133' / W122 38.226'). Continue hiking to a junction.

4.6 Arrive at the junction with the Winter Falls Trail. Continue straight. Stay on the Canyon Trail at any junctions, visiting Middle North Falls (N44 53.343' / W122 38.596'), Drake Falls (N44 53.350' / W122 38.786'), Double Falls (N44 53.517' / W122 38.732'), Lower North Falls (N44 53.466' / W122 38.843'), and Lower South Falls (N44 53.115' / W122 39.702') along the way.

7.7 Stay straight at a junction just before South Falls (N44 52.781 W122 39.498). The paved path then leads behind the falls and ascends back up to the parking area where you started the hike.

8.2 Arrive at the parking area.

30 Shellburg Falls

Perhaps due to the neighboring Silver Falls State Park, the easy-to-access and striking Shellburg Falls garners very little in the way of attention. So if you're in the market for a Trail of Ten Falls–caliber waterfall without the throngs, Shellburg is a great choice. You'll also get to visit two other falls along the way. And even though Lower Shellburg is smaller and the view of Stasel is a bit obscured, they definitely sweeten the pot.

See map on page 108.
Height: Shellburg Falls, 100 feet; Lower Shellburg Falls, 40 feet; Stasel Falls, 125 feet
Distance: 5.6-mile semi-loop
Elevation gain: 850 feet
Difficulty: Moderate
Trail surface: Gravel, hard-packed, rocky
Hiking time: About 2–4 hours

County: Marion
Land status: State forest
Fees and permits: None
Trail contact: Santiam State Forest, (503) 859-2151
Map: *DeLorme Atlas & Gazetteer Oregon*, page 34, C5

Finding the trailhead: From Salem, drive east for 22.5 miles on North Santiam Highway 22. Turn left onto Fern Ridge Road and drive 1.3 miles to a gravel parking area on the right. The hike begins at the locked gate. GPS: N44 48.315' / W122 37.642'

The Hike

Begin by walking up past the locked gate and along a gravel road. The road here is exposed but pleasant, and it is not uncommon to encounter free-roaming cows along this stretch. So those with any bovine-induced anxiety should take heed. Continue the easy ascent for 1.3 miles to a bridge that crosses over Shellburg Creek. Take note of a set of stairs on the left, but continue over the bridge to a small shaded area next to the bridge that affords a view of Lower Shellburg Falls. There are a couple of scramble paths that gain a better vantage, but be careful.

Walk up the previously noted stairs and continue 0.1 mile to a junction with a path down to a viewpoint of Shellburg Falls. In late summer this area is explorable due to the near trickle the creek is reduced to. Come in spring and expect to get a face full of spray. The main path soon leads into a cavern deep behind the falls.

Beyond the falls the path climbs another set of stairs and crosses Shellburg Creek over a footbridge near the top of the falls. The recently rerouted trail meanders toward a campground and emerges on a gravel road. Take a left here and hike 0.1 mile to the campground entrance. Make a right uphill, pass a restroom, and arrive at a junction with the Vine Maple Trail. Make a right onto the trail and hike along a very scenic creek-side path for 0.5 mile to a junction and take a right onto the marked August Mountain Trail.

Shellburg Falls

The view behind Shellburg Falls

Soon the path begins its final climb of 0.4 mile to an intersection with a gravel road. Continue straight for 100 feet and pick up the marked trail again on the right. From here the trail descends as steeply as it climbed for 0.8 mile. After crossing a gravel road on this descent, the trail will encounter the same road a second time. When it does, turn to the left and walk 100 feet to an old road blocked off by a set of large boulders. Walk beyond this set of rocks along the old road for 0.1 mile to a boot path on the right that leads down to a decent, albeit precarious, viewpoint of Stasel Falls.

Walk back out to the gravel road and continue down. After 0.25 mile of hiking, you'll arrive back at Lower Shellburg Falls. Continue down the gravel road and back to the trailhead.

Miles and Directions

0.0 From the trailhead walk up the gravel road and around the locked gate. Continue to a bridge crossing over Shellburg Creek.

1.3 Arrive at Lower Shellburg Falls (N44 48.625' / W122 36.495'). Proceed up the staircase on the north side of the road.

1.4 Arrive at a junction leading to a viewpoint of Shellburg Falls (N44 48.747' / W122 36.513'). Continue along the main trail behind the falls, up another staircase to a gravel road.

1.9 Arrive at a gravel road and make a left. Make a right at the campground entrance.

2.0 Arrive at a junction and make a right onto the Vine Maple Trail. Continue hiking.

2.5 Arrive at a junction and make a right onto the August Mountain Trail. Continue hiking.

2.9 Arrive at a logging road. Walk straight 100 feet and pick up the August Mountain Trail again on the right. Continue hiking downhill. Cross a gravel road, pick up the trail, and then reach the same road a second time.

3.7 Arrive at a gravel road. Turn to the left and walk 100 feet to an old road blocked off by a set of large boulders. Continue past the boulders for 0.1 mile to a boot path on the right leading down to a viewpoint of Stasel Falls (N44 48.544' / W122 36.047'). Return to the gravel road.

4.1 Arrive back at the gravel road and hike back down to the trailhead.

5.6 Arrive back at the trailhead.

31 Henline Falls

An easy add-on to an Opal Creek trip, the short 1.8-mile out-and-back to the impressive 126-foot Henline Falls is a no-brainer if you're in the area and have the energy. Alternately, its size and the numerous waterfalls that hide above it make a trek to Henline worthy of its own day.

Height: 126 feet
Distance: 1.8 miles out and back
Elevation gain: 300 feet
Difficulty: Easy
Trail surface: Hard-packed, rocky
Hiking time: About 1–2 hours
County: Marion

Land status: Wilderness
Fees and permits: None
Trail contact: Detroit Ranger Station, (503) 854-3366
Map: *DeLorme Atlas & Gazetteer Oregon,* page 35, B8

Finding the trailhead: From Salem, drive east on the North Santiam Highway 22 for 23 miles. In the town of Mehama, directly across from the Swiss Village Restaurant, turn left onto Little North Fork Road. Drive 16.3 miles of paved and gravel road to a fork. Go left on FR 2209 and drive 0.2 mile and park at the trailhead on the left. GPS: N44 50.770' / W122 19.502'

The Hike

Getting a real good look at Henline Falls is going to require you to get wet—either from spray in the spring or from wading in the summer. The 126-foot falls expands itself into one broad, angled, curtain-like cascade during high flow. In summer, however, it narrows considerably and primarily sticks to one main slot with some droplets finding their way over the neighboring ledge.

From the trailhead the hike gains elevation steadily but easily, up the remains of an old road. After about a half a mile, the main trail bends around to the left while another path stays straight. Just a few steps after this potentially confusing junction, you'll arrive at a real junction with the Ogle Mountain Trail. Stay straight, continuing along the marked trail toward Henline Falls. Hike another 0.3 mile to the falls.

As you near the base of the falls, you'll encounter some interesting old construction on the trail, remnants of the Silver King Mine operation. Continuing toward the falls, the cave-like opening on the right leads about 30 yards or so before reaching a metal gate that seals off the passage.

For waterfall enthusiasts with good off-trail skills, there is a series of waterfalls known as Maynard Drawson's Family Falls that waits above Henline. Access these falls by taking the Ogle Mountain Trail well above Henline Falls and then making a steep and rugged descent off-trail down to the creek.

Henline Falls

Henline Falls, Opal Creek

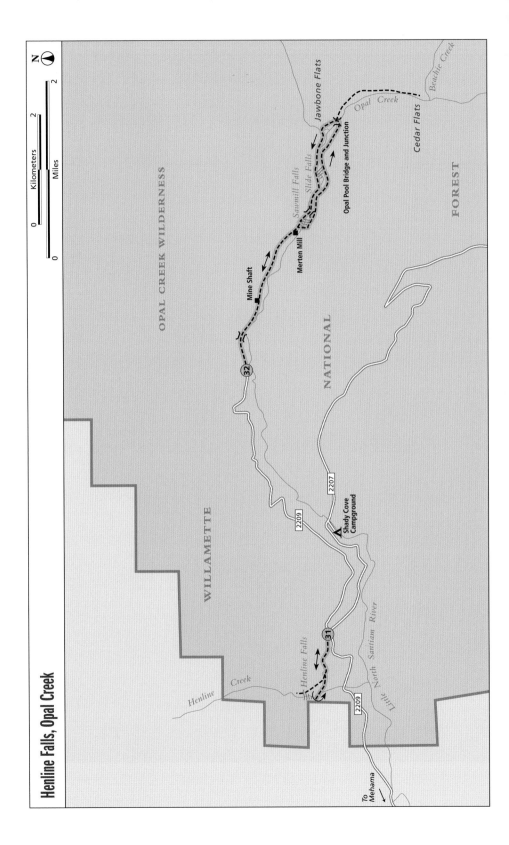

Miles and Directions

0.0 From the trailhead, walk up the old road, now a trail, for half a mile.

0.6 At a split in the road, the trail bends around to the left and soon reaches the junction with the Ogle Mountain Trail. Stay straight, following the signed trail to the falls.

0.9 Arrive at Henline Falls, and head back the way you came.

1.8 Arrive back at the trailhead.

32 Opal Creek

The Opal Creek Wilderness is a low-elevation ancient forest that is home to the largest intact stand of old-growth forest in the western Cascades. Trees in this area can range up to 1,000 years old. Because the forest has remained intact for so long, the flora and fauna interact the way nature intended. Cycles that can take hundreds of years to complete have been left alone to do so, and in the process the forest filters Opal Creek to a state of pristine beauty. Oh, and it has waterfalls!

See map on page 116.
Height: Sawmill Falls, 30 feet; Slide Falls, 20 feet
Distance: 7.4-mile semi-loop or 9.2 mile semi-loop to Cedar Flats
Elevation gain: 800 feet or 1000 feet
Difficulty: Moderate to difficult
Trail surface: Gravel road, hard-packed dirt, rocky, duffy

Hiking time: About 3–7 hours
County: Marion
Land status: Wilderness
Fees and permits: Northwest Forest Pass or small day-use fee required
Trail contact: Detroit Ranger District, (503) 854-3366, www.fs.usda.gov/willamette
Map: *DeLorme Atlas & Gazetteer Oregon,* page 35, B9

Finding the trailhead: To get there, take I-5 South to Salem, exit 253. Head east on OR 22 for 23 miles to the second flashing light in Mehama. Turn left here onto Little North Fork Road and travel 16.3 miles. Fork left onto FR 2209 and drive the final 4.2 miles to the locked gate and trailhead. GPS: N44 51.590' / W122 15.858'

The Hike

If the opportunity to experience a forest in unaltered ancient condition isn't enough, the hike to Opal Creek provides other diversions. The loop hike begins at the gated road to the former mining community of Jawbone Flats (population 9). The town now serves as home to the Opal Creek Ancient Forest Center. The small amount of mining that was done here was performed without chemicals, leaving the watershed undisturbed. Only residents are allowed to drive the road, but fortunately there are some interesting things to see along the walk into town.

Cross a bridge, walk by an old mine shaft, and 2 miles later come to what remains of the Merten Mill. The mill operated briefly during the Great Depression, only clearing a handful of acres before the company's logging trucks fell off of the high canyon road. A trail leads from the mill down to Sawmill Falls and its wonderfully deep, swimmable pool. In another 0.2 mile, cross another bridge and hang a left onto the marked Opal Creek Trail.

The trail is now decidedly different. Note the thickly carpeted forest floor and the softness of the hiking path—a result of thousands of years of forest decay. Up next is Slide Falls. The almost-too-good-to-be-true waterslide takes one quick turn and a

Slide Falls

dip before delivering you into a perfect splash pool. Understand that conditions on Slide Falls vary with the water level, so exercise caution. From here continue to the very deep and vividly colored Opal Pool—a great area for swimming, decorated with a handful of small falls.

For the shorter loop, cross the bridge at Opal Pool and make a left. Head through Jawbone Flats and stay straight back down to the trailhead.

If you're interested in more of the good stuff, cross the bridge and take the trail to the right, continuing upstream. Hike for one more mile, passing more swimmable pools and a couple of mini-cascades before arriving at Cedar Flats, an ancient grove of red cedars that makes for an epic day hike or backpacking trip. Head back the way you came and when you reach the junction at Opal Pool, stay straight and the trail will lead up to a gravel road. Make a left here, walk through Jawbone flats, and follow the gravel road back to the trailhead.

Miles and Directions

0.0 From the gated trailhead, walk 2 miles to the old Merten Mill. Take the broad path that leads through a backpacker's camp and past the abandoned machinery of the mill. Look for a boot path next to an old shelter with a serious lean. Follow this trail down to Sawmill

One of many unnamed cascades and pools along the Opal Creek Trail

Falls. The main trail proceeds another 0.2 mile to a junction (N44 50.967' / W122 13.575').

2.2 Turn right to cross the river over a footbridge, and then make an immediate left onto the Opal Creek Trail. About 0.6 mile from the bridge look for a boot path that leads down to Slide Falls. If it's a hot day and you're up for some nature-made waterpark fun, this is your spot. Continue hiking along the main trail to the signed Opal Pool.

3.6 Arrive at Opal Pool (N44 50.640' / W122 12.377'). To complete the 7.4 mile loop, turn left to cross the creek on a bridge. There are a number of convoluted paths here. Take the trail leading to the left and in about 100 feet it will join an old mining road leading to Jawbone Flats. Follow the road through town and back down to the trailhead. For the longer hike, make a right after crossing the bridge and continue 1 mile upstream to Cedar Flats. Hike back the way you came and at the bridge junction stay straight and the trail will lead up to a gravel road in about 100 feet. Make a left here, walk through Jawbone Flats and follow the gravel road back to the trailhead.

9.2 Arrive back at trailhead.

33 McDowell Creek Falls

McDowell Creek Park is a family-friendly paradise that flies way underneath the radar. It is, however, a stunner of a hike highlighted by a pair of impressive waterfalls and a grotto reminiscent of an Ewok village.

Height: Royal Terrace Falls, 119 feet; Majestic Falls, 39 feet; Crystal Pool Falls, 14 feet
Distance: 1.6-mile loop
Elevation gain: 300 feet
Difficulty: Easy
Trail surface: Gravel, hard-packed dirt, rocky, stairs
Hiking time: About 1–2 hours

County: Linn
Land status: County park
Fees and permits: None
Trail contact: Linn County Parks, (541) 967-3917, http://www.linnparks.com
Map: *DeLorme Atlas & Gazetteer Oregon,* page 40, A5

Finding the trailhead: From the town of Lebanon, take US 20 south 5 miles and turn left at the McDowell Creek Park exit. Follow signs for 9 miles to the first parking area, the Royal Terrace Falls Trailhead. GPS: N44 27.853' / W122 40.940'

The Hike

From the trailhead, hike across a footbridge and continue along the main trail for 0.2 mile to Royal Terrace Falls, where water flows like lacey ribbons over 119 feet and three tiers. Make a left here and cross a bridge that offers the best view of the falls. For the next 0.3 mile, stay right at all junctions, but be careful to avoid boot paths that just lead down to the water.

Cross a road, pick up the trail on the other side and continue hiking through lush forest for a quick 0.2 mile to Crystal Pool Falls. The small but fetching falls fits right in with the feel of the forest. But that mood is about to elevate.

Just a few hundred feet beyond the Crystal Pool, the trail enters a verdant, thickly mossed mini–box canyon. An elevated wooden walkway crosses the creek and delivers you to a viewing platform of Majestic Falls and its fern-laden grotto. Continue up the stairs to an upper viewing area of the falls.

From the upper viewing area, climb another set of steps to the Majestic Falls parking area. Toward the east end of the parking area, the trail resumes. Reenter the woods and hike 0.3 mile to another road crossing. Again, pick up the trail on the other side and hike a very short distance to another junction. Stay left here and hike 0.2 mile to the upper viewpoint of Royal Terrace Falls.

Take a steep set of stairs that leads down the side of the falls and arrive at the first junction of the hike near the bridge at the base of Royal Terrace. Make a left here and return to the trailhead.

McDowell Creek Falls

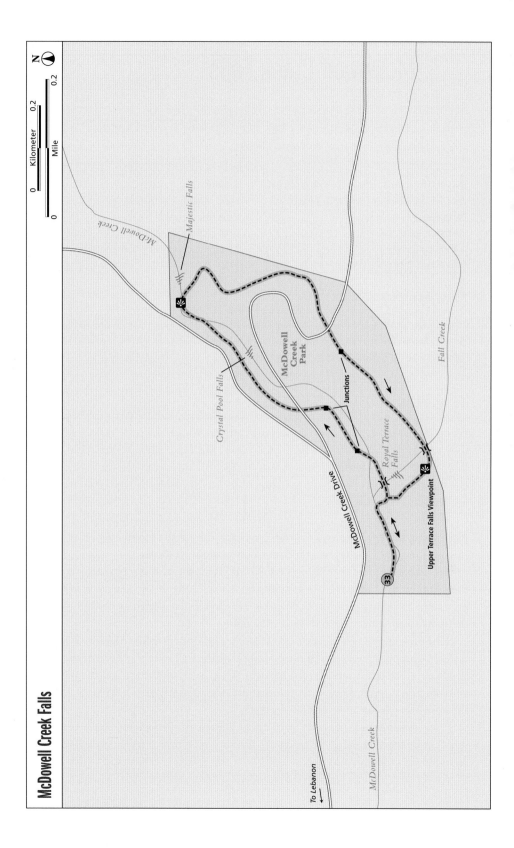

The trail leading to the top of Majestic Falls

Miles and Directions

0.0 From the trailhead, cross a footbridge and arrive at a junction.

0.2 Make a left at the junction and cross a bridge with a view of Royal Terrace Falls (N44 27.823' / W122 40.768'). Make a left after the bridge and stay right at all junctions for 0.3 mile.

0.5 Cross a paved road and continue past Crystal Pool Falls (N44 28.018' / W122 40.559') and Majestic Falls (N44 28.089' / W122 40.463'). Take a set of stairs up to a parking lot and pick up the trail near the east end of the parking area.

0.8 Pick up the trail in the Majestic Falls parking area and continue hiking. Cross another paved road and stay left at a junction leading to the upper viewpoint of Royal Terrace Falls.

1.4 Arrive at the upper viewing area at the top of Royal Terrace Falls. Continue down a set of stairs and make a left. Hike the final 0.2 mile back to the trailhead.

1.6 Arrive back at the trailhead.

34 Lower Soda Falls

For roughly 8,000 years, Native American tribes called this area home. The Cascadia Cave provided shelter for many. Now, the state park serves as home for folks who are leisurely transients in nature. The popular campground and day-use area has a lot to offer. But waterfall lovers will want to make a beeline to a path that starts out paralleling the Cascadia Park Campground and quickly enters into old-growth forest with high-reaching canyon walls populated with Doug firs and western red cedars. Lower Soda Falls itself is a unique cascade that zigzags its way through a basalt crevice before leaping off its final 50-foot plunge.

Height: 134 feet
Distance: 1.4 miles out and back
Elevation gain: 380 feet
Difficulty: Easy
Trail surface: Hard-packed dirt, rocky
Hiking time: About 1 hour
County: Linn

Land status: State park
Fees and permits: None
Trail contact: Oregon State Parks, (800) 551-6949, oregonstateparks.org
Map: *DeLorme Atlas & Gazetteer Oregon,* page 41, A7

Finding the trailhead: From the town of Sweet Home, travel US 20 east for roughly 14 miles. After milepost 41 make a left at the sign for Cascadia State Park. Cross a long bridge and park at the large day-use area next to the restroom. GPS: N44 23.952' / W122 28.845'

Soda Falls

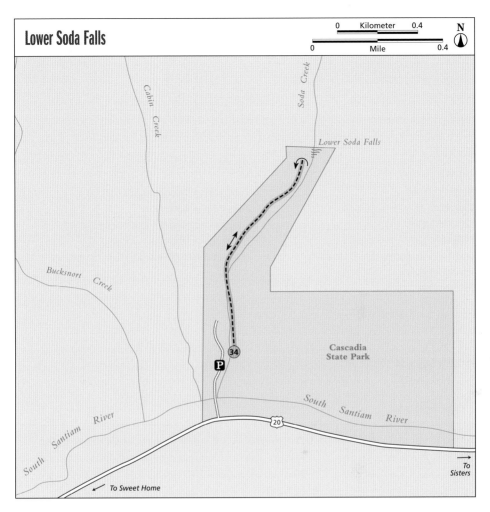

Lower Soda Falls

0 Kilometer 0.4
0 Mile 0.4
N

Cabin Creek

Soda Creek

Lower Soda Falls

Bucksnort Creek

34

P

Cascadia State Park

South Santiam River

South Santiam River

20

To Sisters

To Sweet Home

The Hike

From the day-use parking area, walk up the road about 100 feet and bear right at a fork. Another 100 feet later look for the signed trail to Soda Creek Falls on the left side of the road.

Follow the trail as it briefly skirts by the campground, paralleling the creek. The trail climbs steadily through enchanting old-growth woods for 0.7 mile to Lower Soda Creek Falls. A scramble path leads down to the base of the falls, visiting its shady swimming hole and rocky beach. Return the way you came.

Miles and Directions

0.0 From the marked trailhead, hike 0.7 mile to Lower Soda Falls (N44 24.444' / W122 28.555').

0.7 From the falls, return the way you came.

1.4 Arrive back at the trailhead.

35 House Rock Falls

It may not be the easiest cascade to get a good view of. However, House Rock Falls does offer you the chance to hike along the historic Santiam Wagon Road, stroll through lush old-growth forest, access an exquisite creek with numerous swimming holes, and visit the house-size boulder that once shielded pioneer families from angry weather.

Height: 30 feet
Distance: 2.0-mile semi-loop
Elevation gain: 400 feet
Difficulty: Easy
Trail surface: Hard-packed dirt, rocky
Hiking time: About 1–2 hours
County: Linn

Land status: National forest
Fees and permits: None
Trail contact: Sweet Home Ranger District, (541) 367-5168
Map: *DeLorme Atlas & Gazetteer Oregon,* page 41, B9

Finding the trailhead: From the town of Sweet Home, travel US 20 east for 25 miles. After milepost 54 make a right toward the House Rock Campground. Drive 1.5 miles along gravel FR 2044 to a small pullout and a locked gate on the right side of the road, directly across from a Santiam Wagon Road sign. GPS: N44 23.146' / W122 14.268'

The Hike

Constructed in 1866–67, the Santiam Wagon Road connected the cattle towns of the Willamette Valley with the gold-mining towns of eastern Oregon. Replaced by the road you'll use to get there, US 20, the old wagon road passed into obscurity. Now, sections of the original Santiam Wagon Road have been reborn as trails.

Pass the locked gate, and begin your walk along part of Oregon's history. After 0.4 mile of hiking through pleasant but unremarkable woods, the trail banks sharply to the right and drops into inviting old growth. After 0.7 mile of total hiking, look for a marked side path on the right.

Take this trail down 300 feet to another junction and make a right. Follow the occasionally steep trail for a quick 0.1 mile to the top of House Rock Falls. There are a couple of scramble routes that lead to the bottom of the falls, but you'll probably have to be willing to get wet feet to get a real good look at the falls.

Make your way back up to the previous junction and stay straight, following the trail and the Santiam River for 0.2 mile to the wide-open cave known as House Rock. The trail now circles the massive boulder that provides the cave. Stay left at any junctions and follow the trail a final 1 mile back to the trailhead.

Top: House Rock Falls ▶
Bottom: House Rock Falls trail

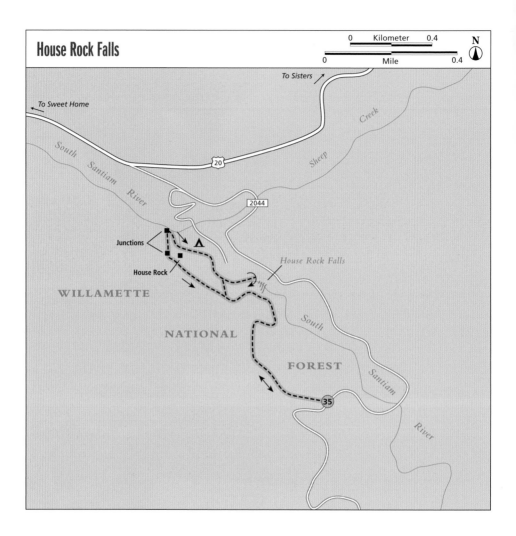

Miles and Directions

0.0 From the locked gate, walk 0.7 mile to a junction.

0.7 Arrive at a junction and go right for 300 feet to a second junction. Make another right and descend down to House Rock Falls (N44 23.509' / W122 14.780').

0.8 Arrive at House Rock Falls. Head back to the previous junction and stay straight.

1.2 Arrive at House Rock. Continue hiking, staying left at any junctions, and return to the trailhead.

2.0 Arrive back at the trailhead.

36 Sahalie/Koosah Falls

This 2.8-mile loop hike visits two massive, thundering waterfalls, a river as comely as you could hope for, and viewpoint after viewpoint.

Height: Sahalie, 73 feet; Koosah, 64 feet
Distance: 2.8-mile loop
Elevation gain: 400 feet
Difficulty: Easy
Trail surface: Paved, hard-packed, rocky
Hiking time: About 1–2 hours
County: Linn

Land status: National forest
Fees and permits: None
Trail contact: McKenzie River Ranger District, (541) 822-3381
Map: *DeLorme Atlas & Gazetteer Oregon,* page 42, B1

Finding the trailhead: From the town of Sisters, take US 20 west for 29 miles and make a left onto OR 126 East. Proceed 200 feet and make a right onto OR 126 West. Drive 5.2 more miles and pull into the Sahalie Falls parking area on the right. GPS: N44 20.900' / W121 59.787'

The Hike

From the parking area, walk a couple hundred feet down to the lower viewpoint of Sahalie Falls. Continue downriver to the left. The water here runs forceful and clean, occasionally swirling in deep blue and green pools.

Sahalie Falls

Koosah Falls

After 0.5 mile you'll pass the equally impressive Koosah Falls. Interestingly, the words *Sahalie* and *Koosah* both mean "high" or "heaven" in Northwest Chinook jargon—fitting descriptions for both. You'll soon encounter a handful of viewpoints, all with great views of the falls and the river. Continue hiking, avoiding any trails that lead up to the left, and arrive at a gravel road 0.4 mile later. Veer to the right here and walk over and past the river about 0.1 mile to a signed trail. Follow this trail for 350 feet to a junction. Turn right onto the McKenzie River Trail.

Continue hiking 1.2 miles along this trail, passing more viewpoints along the way, before arriving at a bridge. Cross over the river and go right. Hike a final 0.5 mile back to the trailhead, passing yet another viewpoint near the top of Sahalie Falls along the way.

Miles and Directions

0.0 From the trailhead, walk a few hundred feet down to a viewpoint of Sahalie Falls (N44 20.907' / W121 59.832'). Continue downriver, avoiding trails leading left, and arrive at Koosah Falls (N44 20.685' / W122 00.022').

0.3 Arrive at Koosah Falls. Continue hiking downriver to a gravel road.

Sahalie/Koosah Falls

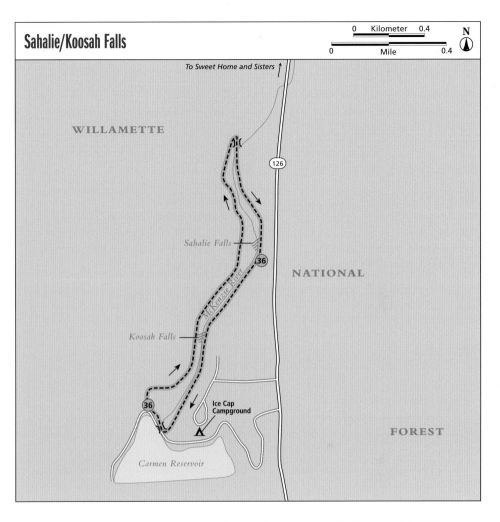

0 Kilometer 0.4
0 Mile 0.4
N

To Sweet Home and Sisters ↑

WILLAMETTE

126

Sahalie Falls

36

NATIONAL

Koosah Falls

36

Ice Cap Campground

FOREST

Carmen Reservoir

0.6 At a gravel road, veer right and walk 0.1 mile to a signed trail. Take this trail for 350 feet to another junction.

1.0 Arrive at a junction with the McKenzie River Trail. Take a right and follow the trail for 1.2 miles.

2.2 Cross a footbridge, make a right, and hike another 0.5 mile back to the trailhead.

2.8 Arrive back at the trailhead.

37 Proxy Falls

One of the true headliners in central Oregon, Proxy Falls is well known for being photogenic, though it can be a struggle to get the whole falls in one shot. And the hike, which leads through a lava field, is an eclectic geological grab bag wrapped up in a tidy 1.6-mile serving.

Height: Upper Proxy Falls, 129 feet; Proxy Falls 226 feet
Distance: 1.6-mile loop
Elevation gain: 200 feet
Difficulty: Easy
Trail surface: Rocky, hard-packed dirt
Hiking time: About 30 minutes to 1.5 hours

County: Lane
Land status: National forest
Fees and permits: None
Trail contact: McKenzie River Ranger District, (541) 822-3381, www.fs.usda.gov/willamette
Map: *DeLorme Atlas & Gazetteer Oregon*, page 42, D2

Finding the trailhead: From the town of Sisters, head west on OR 242 for 27.4 miles to the signed Proxy Falls Trailhead on the left. GPS: N44 10.077' / W121 55.643'

The Hike

From the parking area, start at the westernmost trailhead. The loop is laid out as a one-way only, so just follow the signage. The hike begins with an easy stroll around the base of a lava flow and then climbs on top of it. This exposed section of the hike is utterly fascinating and becomes electric with fall color in late September and early October.

Soon the trail dips into an elfin forest and the character and feel of the whole hike manages to change in about 100 feet. The trail now meanders through a canyon carved by ancient glacial flows. After 0.7 mile you'll arrive at a junction with a side trail leading to Proxy Falls. Take this 0.1-mile scurry down to one of the more awe-inspiring scenes in Oregon. You'll want to take some time here. There is a lot of exploring to do and a seemingly endless number of angles from which to photograph the falls. Bring your water shoes.

After exploring the grandeur that is Proxy Falls, make your way back up to the main trail and continue 0.2 mile to a junction with the path leading to Upper Proxy Falls. The 129-foot upper falls is a dynamo and would be a spectacle anywhere else. Unfortunately for Upper Proxy Falls, her taller and slightly more fetching sister lives only a couple of blocks away.

Once back on the main trail, the path reemerges from the lush forest landscape and leads a final 0.4 mile through the lava flow back to the parking area.

Top: Proxy Falls
Bottom: The trail leading to Proxy Falls

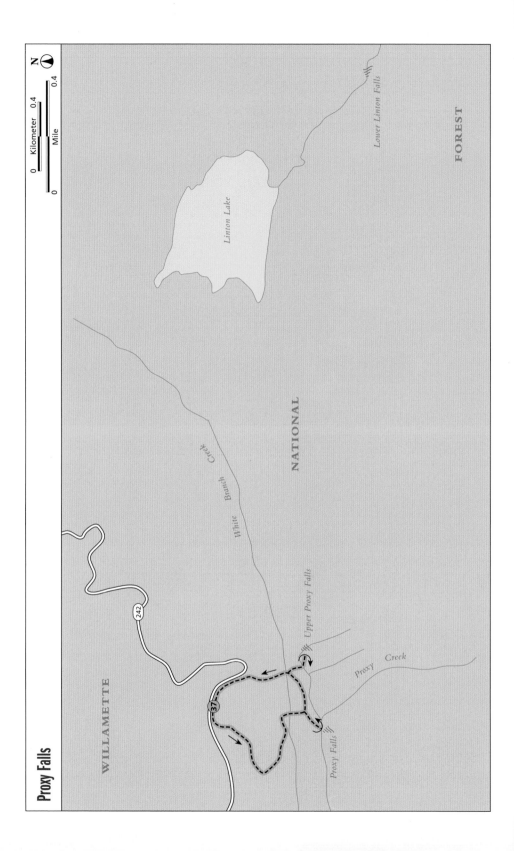

Proxy Falls

WILLAMETTE

NATIONAL

FOREST

Linton Lake

White Branch Creek

Proxy Creek

Upper Proxy Falls

Proxy Falls

Lower Linton Falls

242

37

N

0   Kilometer   0.4

0   Mile   0.4

Miles and Directions

0.0 From the parking area, follow signage and take the westernmost trail leading counterclockwise.

0.7 Arrive at the side trail leading down to Proxy Falls (N44 09.758' / W121 55.725'). Continue along the main trail.

1.1 Arrive at a side trail leading to Upper Proxy Falls (N44 09.798' /W121 55.440'). Continue hiking back to the parking area.

1.6 Arrive back at the parking area.

38 Steelhead Falls

This hike showcases classic central Oregon landscape dotted with sagebrush and guarded by hoodoos. A deep basalt canyon carved out by the Deschutes River plays home to the 1-mile round-trip trek to Steelhead Falls. Not known for cascades that exceed little more than glorified rapids, the Deschutes tumbles over 18-foot Steelhead Falls in a three-pronged plunge that is as noteworthy as 18 feet can get.

Height: 18 feet
Distance: 1.0 mile out and back
Elevation gain: 150 feet
Difficulty: Easy
Trail surface: Dirt, rocky
Hiking time: About 30 minutes
County: Jefferson

Land status: National grassland
Fees and permits: None
Trail contact: Crooked River National Grassland, (541) 475-9272, http://www.fs.usda.gov/centraloregon
Map: *DeLorme Atlas & Gazetteer Oregon,* page 43, A8

Finding the trailhead: From the town of Redmond, take US 97 north for 6 miles through the town of Terrebonne. Make a left onto NW Lower Bridge Way, toward the Crooked River Ranch. There are a lot of twists and turns here, but the signage to the falls is excellent. Drive 2.1 miles and turn right onto NW 43rd Street. Continue 1.9 miles and make a left onto NW Chinook Avenue. Drive 1.1 miles and turn left onto Badger Road. Drive 1.8 miles and turn right onto Quail Road. Drive 1.2 miles and turn left onto River Road. Drive 1 mile to the end of the road and the parking area. GPS: N44 24.672' / W121 17.558'

The Hike

The trail begins on the right side of the parking area near a placard and ambles easily toward the river a short way before steeply descending to the water. The main trail can be a little tough to differentiate from a number of boot paths that lead down to the water. Explore at your leisure, but know that the main trail follows a pretty steady trajectory paralleling the river.

After 0.5 mile you'll reach the falls and a couple of nice viewpoints and access areas. Note that on weekends and hot

Steelhead Falls

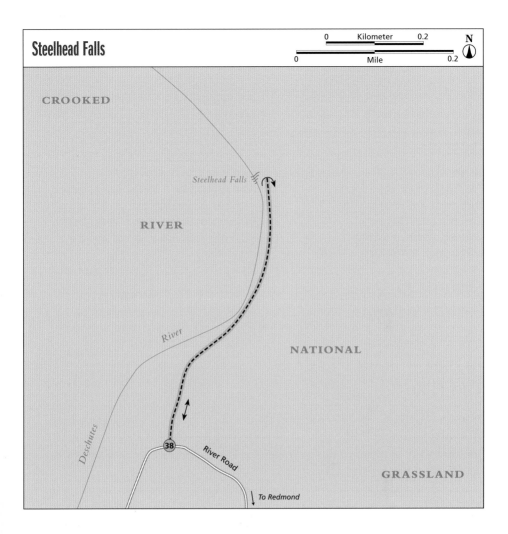

Steelhead Falls

CROOKED

Steelhead Falls

RIVER

River

NATIONAL

Deschutes

38

River Road

GRASSLAND

To Redmond

summer days, this area attracts a party. So don't expect a whole lot of solitude under those conditions. Head back the way you came to complete the hike.

Miles and Directions

0.0 From the trailhead, hike 0.5 mile to Steelhead Falls (N44 24.984' / W121 17.370').

0.5 Arrive at Steelhead Falls. Head back the way you came.

1.0 Arrive back at the trailhead.

39 Tumalo Falls

This is one of the premier hikes in Oregon for waterfall lovers. At least three sizable cascades and as many as a dozen smaller falls populate the scenic creeks along the way. And it is all highlighted by the massive Tumalo.

Height: Tumalo Falls, 90 feet; Double Falls, 89 feet; Bridge Creek Falls, 25 feet
Distance: 7.4-mile loop
Elevation gain: 700 feet
Difficulty: Moderate to difficult
Trail surface: Gravel, hard-packed dirt, rocky
Hiking time: About 2.5–5 hours
County: Deschutes

Land status: National forest
Fees and permits: Northwest Forest Pass or small day-use fee required
Trail contact: Bend–Fort Rock Ranger District, (541) 583-4000, http://www.fs.usda.gov/centraloregon
Map: *DeLorme Atlas & Gazetteer Oregon,* page 43, F6

Finding the trailhead: From Bend, take Tumalo Avenue west for 10.3 miles. Along the way the road will become Galveston, then Skyliner. Turn right onto gravel FR 4603 and drive 2.5 more miles to the large Tumalo Falls parking area. GPS: N44 01.920' / W121 33.984'

The Hike

From the trailhead near the restrooms, climb a short way to a very popular lower viewpoint of Tumalo Falls. Lighting can be tricky here, so unless it's an overcast day, you may want to return to this spot after the hike to try pictures in full afternoon light.

Continue along the main path, and a short distance later, stay right at a junction. The forest here is rather new, having recovered from a 1979 forest fire. But the rebirth is coming along swimmingly. After 0.2 mile you'll reach the large, railed upper viewpoint of Tumalo. Proceed up the main trail, keeping an eye out for mountain bikers, who enjoy this section just as much as hikers. After just under another mile of hiking, you'll arrive at Double Falls, dropping a total of 89 feet.

The next 2.5 miles ascends through denser forest and passes a half a dozen falls, many requiring a quick scramble to the creek to get an optimal view. At a junction turn left. You're now entering the Bridge Creek Watershed, which serves as the main source of drinking water for the city of Bend. So no dogs, no bikes, no camping. The trail also leaves the water here for 0.3 mile until the trail reaches a creek crossing with no bridge. Get wet if you like, but a downed tree serves as a fairly stable and safe alternative.

From the creek crossing, enjoy a steady descent for 2.1 miles to a junction. Make a left here and in 0.4 mile you'll pass Bridge Creek Falls. Continue the final 0.9 mile back to the parking area.

Tumalo Falls

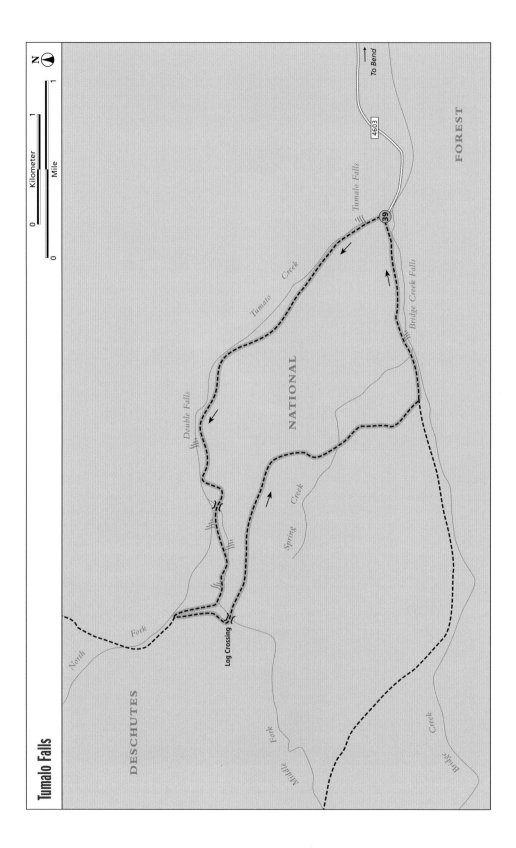

Tumalo Falls

N

0   1   Kilometer
0   1   Mile

DESCHUTES

North   Fork

Double Falls

Tumalo   Creek

NATIONAL

Log Crossing

Middle   Fork

Spring   Creek

Bridge Creek Falls

Tumalo Falls

39

4603

To Bend

FOREST

Bridge   Creek

Miles and Directions

0.0 From the trailhead, hike upstream, visiting two viewpoints of Tumalo Falls (N44 02.020' / W121 34.025'). Stay right at any junctions.

1.0 Arrive at Double Falls (N44 02.517' / W121 34.745'). Continue along the main trail, taking in numerous smaller cascades.

2.5 Cross a footbridge and continue hiking, passing even more falls.

3.7 Arrive at a junction. Turn left onto the Swampy Lakes Trail.

4.0 Arrive at a creek crossing. A downed tree here works well.

6.1 Arrive at a junction. Make a left and continue hiking.

6.5 Arrive at Bridge Creek Falls (GPS: N44 01.830' / W121 34.795'). Continue up the trail.

7.4 Arrive back at the trailhead.

40 Spirit Falls

The following trio of photogenic waterfalls are all within a handful of miles of one another in the Umpqua National Forest. If you have the time, you should really hit all three in the same go. All three offer solitude and two provide wonderful picnic options. As an added bonus, foolproof signage and excellent gravel roads help make these remote falls a joy to visit. The first of the three is Spirit Falls.

Height: 40 feet
Distance: 0.6 mile out and back
Elevation gain: 200 feet
Difficulty: Easy
Trail surface: Hard-packed dirt, rocky
Hiking time: About 30 minutes
County: Lane
Land status: National forest

Fees and permits: None
Trail contact: Cottage Grove Ranger District, (541) 767-5000, http://www.fs.usda.gov/recarea/umpqua/null/recarea/?recid=63376&actid=24
Map: *DeLorme Atlas & Gazetteer Oregon,* page 47, C10

Finding the trailhead: From I-5 south of Eugene, take exit 174 east toward Dorena Lake. At 18.5 miles from I-5, make a slight left onto FR 17 (also known as Layng Creek Road). Drive 8.7 miles to where the pavement ends and turn right onto gravel FR 1790. Drive 0.2 mile to a small pullout and the Spirit Falls trailhead on the right. GPS: N43 43.888' / W122 38.379'

The Hike

From the trailhead, descend 200 feet over 0.3 mile to where Alex Creek tumbles over a 40-foot cliff as Spirit Falls. The area that extends out from the base of the falls is a joy to take in. A well-placed picnic bench and peaceful grotto make Spirit Falls a place where you can spend a considerable amount of time. The falls themselves, like many in the Umpqua National Forest, take on a wildly different appearance based on time of year and water flow. For Spirit Falls, all are appealing. Please note that this watershed is what provides Cottage Grove with its water supply, so no camping or swimming is allowed.

Miles and Directions

0.0 From the trailhead, hike 0.3 mile down to the base of the falls.
0.3 Arrive at Spirit Falls (GPS: N43 43.857' / W122 38.612'). Head back the way you came.
0.6 Arrive back at the trailhead.

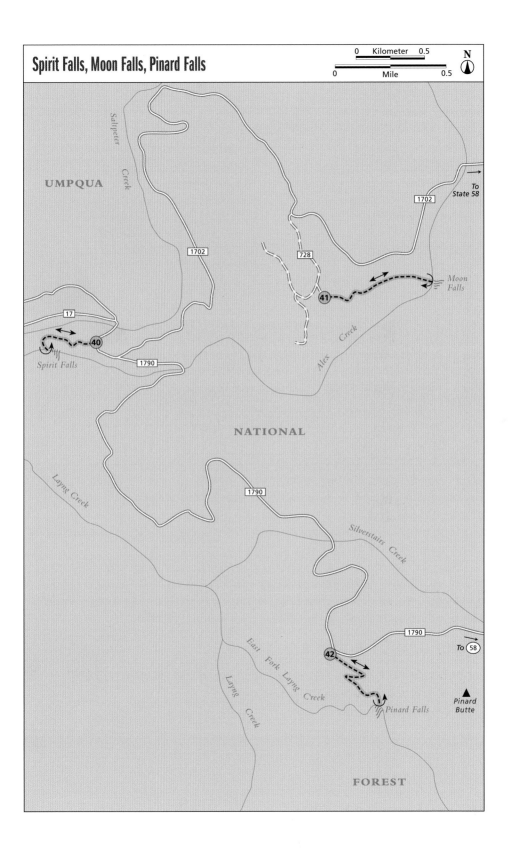

Spirit Falls, Moon Falls, Pinard Falls

UMPQUA

Salpeter Creek

1702

1702

To State 58

728

41

Moon Falls

17

40

Spirit Falls

1790

Alex Creek

NATIONAL

Layng Creek

1790

Silverstairs Creek

1790

To 58

42

East Fork Layng Creek

Layng Creek

Pinard Falls

Pinard Butte

FOREST

41 Moon Falls

The same creek that produces Spirit Falls downstream produces the striking Moon Falls. And just like Spirit Falls, Moon Falls is a great spot for a picnic break.

See map on page 143.
Height: 100 feet
Distance: 1.0 mile out and back
Elevation gain: 160 feet
Difficulty: Easy
Trail surface: Old road bed, hard-packed dirt, rocky
Hiking time: About 30 minutes to 1 hour
County: Lane

Land status: National forest
Fees and permits: None
Trail contact: Cottage Grove Ranger District, (541) 767-5000, http://www .fs.usda.gov/recarea/umpqua/null/ recarea/?recid=63376&actid=24
Map: *DeLorme Atlas & Gazetteer Oregon*, page 47, C10

Finding the trailhead: From I-5 south of Eugene, take exit 174 east toward Dorena Lake. At 18.5 miles from I-5, make a slight left onto FR 17 (also known as Layng Creek Road). Drive 8.7 miles to where the pavement ends and turn right onto gravel FR 1790. Drive 0.3 mile and turn left onto FR 1702. Drive 2.7 more miles and make a right onto a slightly rougher road, FR 728, and drive 0.3 mile to the road's end and the parking area for Moon Falls. GPS: N43 44.049' / W122 37.218'

The Hike

From the parking area, the trail briefly follows an old road before becoming a more traditional trail. The path leads through very young forest for almost the entire 0.5 mile to the falls. However, just when the falls get within earshot, the trail banks sharply to the left and delivers you into a stunningly beautiful old-growth canyon that hides another perfectly placed picnic bench.

Moon Falls spreads out and veils across a broad wall of basalt for nearly 100 feet. It then collects itself and plunges in side-by-side falls that crash into mossy boulders, becoming Alex Creek again. Please note that this watershed is what provides Cottage Grove with its water supply, so no camping or swimming is allowed.

Miles and Directions

0.0 From the trailhead, hike 0.5 mile to the base of Moon Falls (N43 44.109 W122 36.667).
0.5 Arrive at the falls. Head back the way you came.
1.0 Arrive back at the trailhead.

Moon Falls

42 Pinard Falls

Another stately cascade, Pinard Falls drops through a narrow slot before broadening slightly and falling gracefully over 100 feet to a semi-hidden pool below. Flanked by moss-covered rock and drooping cedars, it's hard not to take pause to admire this cascade.

See map on page 143.
Height: 105 feet
Distance: 1.0 mile out and back
Elevation gain: 330 feet
Difficulty: Easy
Trail surface: Old road bed, hard-packed dirt, rocky
Hiking time: About 30 minutes to 1 hour
County: Lane

Land status: National forest
Fees and permits: None
Trail contact: Cottage Grove Ranger District, (541) 767-5000, http://www .fs.usda.gov/recarea/umpqua/null/ recarea/?recid=63376&actid=24
Map: *DeLorme Atlas & Gazetteer Oregon,* page 47, C10

Finding the trailhead: From I-5 south of Eugene, take exit 174 east toward Dorena Lake. At 18.5 miles from I-5, make a slight left onto FR 17 (also known as Layng Creek Road). Drive 8.7 miles to where the pavement ends and turn right onto gravel FR 1790. Drive 3.3 miles to a signed pullout on the right for Pinard Falls. GPS: N43 42.786' / W122 37.190'

The Hike

Just like Moon Falls, the trail leading to Pinard starts out along an old roadbed for 0.3 mile. Then a well-signed trail drops steeply down to the left for another 0.2 mile to a set of stairs and a couple of good views of the falls. Unfortunately, there is no real spot for a picnic here. A steep scramble gains access to the area at the bottom of the falls. But again, bear in mind that swimming is not allowed in this watershed that supplies Cottage Grove.

Miles and Directions

0.0 From the trailhead, follow an old roadbed for 0.3 mile.

0.3 Arrive at a signed trail marker leading sharply down to the left. Take this and continue down to the falls.

0.5 Arrive at a viewpoint for Pinard Falls (N43 42.613' / W122 36.935'). Return the way you came.

1.0 Arrive back at the trailhead.

Pinard Falls

43 Trestle Creek Falls

A thoroughly delightful trek through old-growth forest leads to a pair of the best waterfall grottos in the Umpqua National Forest: Trestle and Upper Trestle Creek Falls.

Height: Upper Trestle Creek Falls, 70 feet (combined drops); Trestle Creek Falls, 45 feet
Distance: 4.0-mile loop
Elevation gain: 850 feet
Difficulty: Easy to moderate
Trail surface: Hard-packed dirt, rocky
Hiking time: About 1.5–3 hours
County: Lane

Land status: National forest
Fees and permits: None
Trail contact: Cottage Grove Ranger District, (541) 767-5000, http://www.fs.usda.gov/recarea/umpqua/null/recarea/?recid=63376&actid=24
Map: *DeLorme Atlas & Gazetteer Oregon*, page 47, D10

Finding the trailhead: From I-5 south of Eugene, take exit 174 east toward Dorena Lake. At 18.5 miles from I-5, stay straight on Brice Creek Road (FR 22) and drive 8.2 miles to the Brice/Champion Creek trailhead pullout on the left. GPS: N43 38.503' / W122 39.521'

The Hike

From the parking area, walk across a bridge that passes over Brice Creek and veer right for about 50 feet to a signed trail. The trail climbs steadily for 1.5 miles, passing through stands of old growth before arriving at Upper Trestle Creek Falls. This two-tiered gem of a cascade resides in a captivating alcove of ferns and mosses. The falls can be reduced to a robust seep by late summer, but it is still a sight to behold even under low-water conditions. The trail leads behind the upper tier of the falls before rounding a corner and descending 1.1 mile to a junction with the Brice Creek Trail.

Make a left onto the Brice Creek Trail and hike 0.3 mile to a bridge and a marked trail on the left leading to Trestle Creek Falls. Follow this trail 0.3 mile to the falls. While smaller in stature than the upper cascade, Trestle Creek Falls is just as pleasing. The falls spill into a narrow gorge decorated with abundant vegetation and downed trees strewn about like matchsticks.

Continue back to the main trail and head the final 0.3 mile back to the trailhead.

Miles and Directions

0.0 From the parking area, cross a bridge and walk up the road for 50 feet to a marked trail on the left. Take this steadily ascending trail to Upper Trestle Creek Falls (N43 39.053' / W122 39.074').

1.5 Arrive at Upper Trestle Creek Falls. Continue hiking.

Upper Trestle Creek Falls

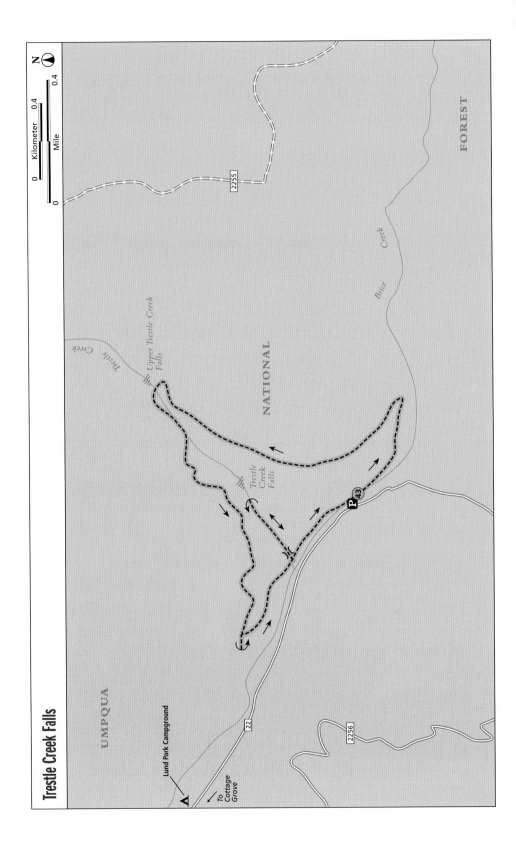

Trestle Creek Falls

UMPQUA

NATIONAL

FOREST

Lund Park Campground

To Cottage Grove

22

2255

2256

Trestle Creek

Upper Trestle Creek Falls

Trestle Creek Falls

Brice Creek

P 43

N

Kilometer
0   0.4

Mile
0   0.4

2.7 Arrive at a junction with the Brice Creek Trail and make a left.

3.0 Arrive at a junction with a side trail leading to Trestle Creek Falls (N43 38.814' / W122 39.521'). Take this path up to the falls and return to the main trail. Make a left and continue hiking back to the parking area.

4.0 Arrive back at the parking area.

Trestle Creek Falls

44 Lillian Falls

Don't expect any dramatic plunges here. Lillian Falls is a true cascade-style waterfall, tumbling slowly and gradually over a series of rocks and boulders for roughly 70 to 100 feet. Along the way, however, you can expect to be stopped in your tracks by ancient stands of old growth.

Height: 70 feet
Distance: 2.4 miles out and back
Elevation gain: 580 feet
Difficulty: Easy
Trail surface: Hard-packed dirt, rocky
Hiking time: About 1–2 hours
County: Lane
Land status: National forest

Fees and permits: None
Trail contact: Middle Fork Ranger District, (541) 782-2283, http://www.fs.usda.gov/detail/willamette/home/?cid=stelprdb5136473
Map: *DeLorme Atlas & Gazetteer Oregon,* page 48, D5 and 49 D6

Finding the trailhead: From the town of Oakridge, turn north off of OR 58 at a traffic light onto Crestview Road. Drive 0.2 mile and make a right onto First Street. Drive through the old downtown and continue onto Salmon Creek Road / FR 24. After 11.2 miles stay right at a fork to continue on FR 24. After 2.8 miles stay left at a fork, continuing onto gravel FR 2421. Drive another 8.6 very bumpy miles to the end of the road and the trailhead. GPS: N43 42.166' / W122 06.726'

The Hike

From the trailhead, climb steadily for 1.2 miles to a spot where the trail reaches a creek, switches back sharply to the left, and launches up. At the switchback walk off trail and down to the creek and the base of Lillian Falls.

There's no good spot to get a look at the whole thing, so take in what you can and enjoy the walk back to the trailhead.

Miles and Directions

0.0 From the trailhead, hike 1.2 miles to a switchback at Nettie Creek. Here, walk down to the creek and the base of Lillian Falls (N43 41.880' / W122 05.549').

1.2 From Lillian Falls, walk back the way you came.

2.4 Arrive back at the trailhead.

Lillian Falls

Lillian Falls

WILLAMETTE

To Oakridge

2421

44

NATIONAL

Black Creek

Nettie Creek

Lillian Falls

FOREST

Bongo Lake

0   Kilometer   0.4
0   Mile   0.4

N

The author on Lillian Falls trail

45 Salt Creek Falls

Though the impressive 286-foot Salt Creek Falls is the star of the show, a rhododendron-rich trail leads to another notable falls in the area: Diamond Creek Falls. In addition, the complete hike provides a thigh-burning climb to Fall Creek Falls.

Height: Salt Creek Falls, 286 feet; Diamond Creek Falls, 120 feet; Fall Creek Falls, 160 feet (combined drops)
Distance: 3.4-mile loop or 6.0-mile semi-loop
Elevation gain: 400 feet or 1,350 feet
Difficulty: Moderate to difficult
Trail surface: Hard-packed dirt, rocky
Hiking time: About 2.5-4 hours
County: Lane

Land status: National forest
Fees and permits: Northwest Forest Pass or small day-use fee required
Trail contact: Middle Fork Ranger District, (541) 782-2283, http://www.fs.usda.gov/detail/willamette/home/?cid=stelprdb5136473
Map: *DeLorme Atlas & Gazetteer Oregon*, page 48, E5

Finding the trailhead: From the town of Oakridge, take OR 58 east for 21.5 miles, 1 mile east of the highway tunnel, to a signed turnout for Salt Creek Falls on the right. Follow the road down to a large parking area near restrooms and a kiosk. GPS: N43 36.713' / W122 07.674'

The Hike

Walk past the interpretive kiosk to a fenced viewing area and overlook of Salt Creek Falls. At nearly 300 feet, it's one of the tallest accessible falls in Oregon. To get a better look, follow an unpaved boot path to the right of the viewing platform. The trail leads steeply down to the base of Salt Creek Falls.

To begin the loop hike, go back to the kiosk/restroom area and take the paved walkway upstream about 300 feet to a signed trail. Turn right onto the path; walk past a picnic area and cross Salt Creek on a footbridge. After the bridge follow a faint path into the woods for 300 feet to a signed junction.

Turn right at the junction and climb a quick 0.2 mile to a wide-open canyon view. Continue along the main trail, past Too Much Bear Lake and a number of spur paths to optional viewpoints, for 1.1 mile to a junction leading down to Diamond Creek Falls. The steep path gets down the canyon wall in a hurry, crosses a footbridge, and in 0.2 mile ends at the base of the spectacular Diamond Creek Falls. The veiling, horsetail-style falls spreads wide and descends 120 feet over basalt steps and fissures. Because of its unique layout, the falls are unusually accessible. During summer water levels, it is possible to safely rock-hop out to the base and feel its power up close.

Make your way back up to the main trail and turn right. At 350 feet you'll reach an upper viewpoint of Diamond Creek Falls that offers a different perspective and a view of where you probably just had a snack and took pictures.

Salt Creek Falls

Diamond Creek Falls

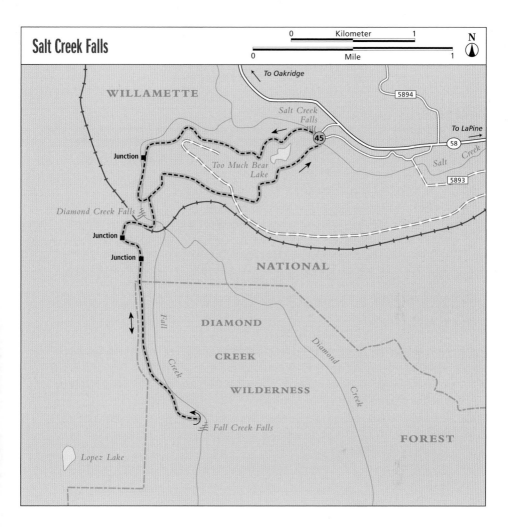

WILLAMETTE

To Oakridge

Salt Creek
Falls

5894

To LaPine

58

Junction

Too Much Bear
Lake

45

Salt   Creek

5893

Diamond Creek Falls

Junction

Junction

NATIONAL

DIAMOND

Fall

CREEK

Diamond

Creek

WILDERNESS

Creek

Fall Creek Falls

FOREST

Lopez Lake

To take the short loop, continue past the upper viewpoint another few hundred feet to a junction. Take a left here and follow the main trail as it makes an easy 1.2-mile descent back to the parking area, crossing a gravel road twice in the process.

To continue on to Fall Creek Falls, walk past this junction for 0.1 mile to a cement bridge crossing Diamond Creek. Just over the bridge, pick up the marked trail on the left and enter the woods again for 0.1 mile. The trail then reemerges from the trees at a railroad crossing. Cross the tracks (carefully) and stay straight along a broad path for 400 feet to a T junction. Turn left here and descend down another broad, rocky path for 0.2 mile to a junction on the right.

Turn right and begin a steady, often very steep climb into the Diamond Creek Wilderness. After 0.8 mile you'll reach a partial view of Fall Creek Falls. Continue another 0.2 mile to a clearer ledge viewpoint of the falls.

From Fall Creek Falls, backtrack 1.4 mile to the junction near the upper viewpoint of Diamond Creek Falls. Hang a right here and follow the trail as it makes an easy 1.2-mile descent back to the parking area, crossing a gravel road twice in the process.

Miles and Directions

0.0 From the parking area, proceed to the Salt Creek Falls viewpoint. To take the loop hike, walk upstream along a paved path for 300 feet to a signed trailhead. Follow this path across a bridge and into the woods.

0.2 Arrive at a signed junction and take a right.

1.4 Arrive at a junction leading down to Diamond Creek Falls (N43 36.441' / W122 08.647'). Take the side path down to enjoy the falls. Once back at the main trail, continue a short way, passing an upper viewpoint of the falls and arriving at a junction. To do the 3.4-mile loop, turn left here and follow the trail 1.2 miles back to the parking area, crossing a gravel road twice in the process. To continue the 6-mile semi-loop, stay straight at the junction. Cross a concrete bridge and pick up the trail on the left. Follow the path through the woods and a short time later arrive at a set of railroad tracks.

2.2 Cross the railroad tracks and continue straight for 400 feet to a T junction. Turn left here and continue hiking 0.2 mile to a junction on the right.

2.4 Arrive at a junction on the right leading up into the Diamond Creek Wilderness. Continue hiking.

3.4 Arrive at a ledged viewpoint of Fall Creek Falls (N43 35.548' / W122 08.349'). Backtrack to the junction just above the upper viewpoint of Diamond Creek Falls.

4.8 Arrive at a junction and turn right. Continue hiking. You'll cross two gravel roads in the process.

6.0 Arrive back at the trailhead.

Honorable Mentions

J. Three Pools

Let's not pretend. The handful of very small drops at the Three Pools Day-Use Area are hardly going to qualify as waterfalls in anyone's book. But this epic series of swimming holes across the street from the Henline Falls Trailhead and a few miles from the Opal Creek Trailhead will be calling you after either of those hikes.

To visit Three Pools from Salem, drive east on the North Santiam Highway 22 for 23 miles. In the town of Mehama, directly across from the Swiss Village Restaurant, turn left onto Little North Fork Road. Drive 16.3 miles of paved and gravel road to a fork. Go left on FR 2209 and drive 0.2 mile to a signed junction for the Three Pools on the right. Drive 1 more mile to the large paved parking area (N44 50.409' / W122 18.743'). A Northwest Forest Pass or small day-use fee is required.

Opal Pool at the Three Pools day use area

K. Salmon Falls

At 25 feet, Salmon Falls is the largest on the north fork of the Santiam River. Splitting into an attractive side-by-side cascade, the falls are conveniently located just off the road on the way up to Opal Creek.

From Salem, drive east on the North Santiam Highway 22 for 23 miles. In the town of Mehama, directly across from the Swiss Village Restaurant, turn left onto Little North Fork Road. Drive 13.5 miles to the Salmon River Falls County Park on the right (N44 49.948' / W122 22.215').

L. Linton Falls

Linton Falls is perhaps one of the largest cascades in the state. However, getting a good look at it can be rather difficult. There is no official or maintained trail to the falls, and it's not possible to see the entire thing from any vantage. While the somewhat accessible lower falls drops an estimated 85 feet, it's believed that the whole thing tumbles over 600 total feet. A portion of the falls can be seen from Linton Lake.

To visit these falls, from the town of Sisters, drive OR 242 west for 25.5 miles to a parking area at the Alder Springs campground. Follow the marked trail 1.5 miles up to Linton Lake and the end of the official trail at Obsidian Creek (N44 10.128' / W121 53.484'). From here a boot path continues around the lake, meeting with Linton Creek. A faint trail climbs from here up toward the falls. The trail becomes less of a trail and more difficult the higher it goes. Only hikers with off-trail experience should attempt to access the falls.

M. Chush Falls

At a thundering 67 feet high and 80 feet wide, Chush Falls is a worthy goal. On top of that, an unmaintained but easily navigable trail leads a short distance beyond the Chush viewpoint to a middle and upper falls. The area now bears the scars of the Pole Creek Fire, which also permanently re-routed and lengthened the hike to a 5-mile out and back.

To visit Chush Falls from the town of Sisters, take FR 16 toward Three Creek Lake for 7 miles. Turn right onto FR 1514, drive 5 miles to FR 600, and turn left just before a bridge crosses Whychus Creek. Drive a short way to the end of the road and the new trailhead.

N. Paulina Creek Falls

If you're visiting the Newberry National Volcanic Monument, it's worth taking a very quick side trip to Paulina Creek Falls' 80-foot twin cascades.

To visit the falls from Bend, take US 97 south for 23 miles and take a left onto Paulina Creek Road. Drive 12.4 more miles to the signed parking area for the falls on the left. From the parking area (N43 42.652' / W121 16.991'), walk a short way to visit a couple different views of the falls.

GOOD PLANTS, BAD PLANTS

While hiking, there are plants you'll want to avoid and plants that can be helpful. Devil's club is a tall plant that grows thorns from its stems and leaves, making it easy to identify. Luckily, few Oregon trails lead through patches of devil's club, so it's also easy to avoid.

Poison oak, typically found in dryer locations, can take on many appearances. It can be shiny and a lustrous green color, or dry with the color of fall foliage. It can present as groundcover, a shrub, or even a vine; and it can be downright good looking. But it's important to be able to identify and avoid it. If ever in doubt, the adage "Leaves of three, let it be" is pretty sage advice.

Conversely the large, soft leaves of the thimbleberry plant, which are slightly reminiscent of devil's club, are not only thorn-free, they are hypoallergenic and very soft. So soft that they are commonly employed as toilet tissue by hikers and have the well-earned moniker "backpackers' TP." Related to the raspberry, thimbleberry plants produce a red, edible berry in summer.

Some plants can be both good and bad. The stinging hairs found on the leaves and stems of stinging nettles can cause a great deal of discomfort. They inject a histamine into the body causing inflammation and pain. On the flip side, the plant has been used for centuries to cure a variety of ailments from arthritis to dandruff, and has also been used as a food source by various Native American tribes.

Fern Falls (Hike 46)

Southern Oregon Cascades

Camping and Accommodations

Historic Prospect Hotel: The Prospect is an incredibly charming B&B and motel all on the same grounds. The Prospect is also a stone's throw or a short drive away from numerous southern Oregon waterfalls. 391 Mill Creek Dr., Prospect, OR 97536; (541) 560-3664; http://www.prospecthotel.com

River Vista Vacation Homes: Located on the banks of one of the Umpqua River's most heralded fishing holes, the River Vista Vacation Homes are also a perfectly located HQ for exploring the waterfalls of the Umpqua River. (541) 496-0506, river vista-vacationhomes.com

Hemlock Lake Campground: Nine sites, $10 a night. Hemlock Falls is located at the campground, and Yakso and Clover Trailheads are across the street. (503) 668-1700

Natural Bridges Campground: Seventeen sites, $10 a site. (541) 618-2200

Whitehorse Falls Campground: Five sites, $10 a night. Whitehorse Falls is directly next to the camping area. (541) 957-3200

46 Fern Falls

The aptly named Fern Falls is by no definition a major cascade. And by late summer expect very low flow. But the hike, which parallels the Umpqua River, is pleasant, and the falls themselves possess a delicate beauty. Viewed from a footbridge, Fern Falls splits, creating two streams that tumble over moss-covered basalt before joining forces again and completing the journey to the Umpqua.

Height: Fern Falls, 40 feet; Deadline Falls, 12 feet
Distance: 3.2 miles out and back
Elevation gain: 500 feet
Difficulty: Easy
Trail surface: Hard-packed dirt, rocky
Hiking time: About 1-2 hours
County: Douglas

Land status: County park
Fees and permits: None
Trail contact: BLM in Roseburg, (541) 440-4930, http://www.blm.gov/or/districts/roseburg/index.php
Map: *DeLorme Atlas & Gazetteer Oregon,* page 54, B3

Finding the trailhead: From Roseburg, take exit 124 and drive east along OR 138 for 22 miles. At a sign for Swiftwater Park, turn right, crossing a bridge over the Umpqua River. Just past the bridge, park at the Tioga Trailhead on the left. GPS: N43 19.894' / W123 00.290'

The Hike

From the trailhead, hike 0.2 mile to a junction. Follow the path leading left down to the Umpqua River and a viewpoint of Deadline Falls. At only 12 feet, its size is not what makes it so popular—it's the salmon leaping up the falls on their way to spawn. After taking in Deadline, return to the main trail and continue upriver.

In a matter of feet, another path leads down to the river. This is a good spot for a snack on the way back. The path now ambles through scenic forest and crosses a number of footbridges. Staying straight at any junctions, continue another 1.4 miles to the long footbridge that crosses a creek at Fern Falls. This is the turnaround point, so when you're good and ready, head back the way you came.

Miles and Directions

0.0 From the trailhead, hike 0.2 mile to a junction.

0.2 Take the path leading left, down to a viewpoint of Deadline Falls (N43 19.830' / W123 00.130'). Return to the main trail and make a left, continuing upriver.

1.6 Arrive at a long footbridge and the viewpoint for Fern Falls (N43 19.188' / W122 59.291'). Head back the way you came.

3.2 Arrive back at the trailhead.

Fern Falls, Susan Creek Falls, Fall Creek Falls

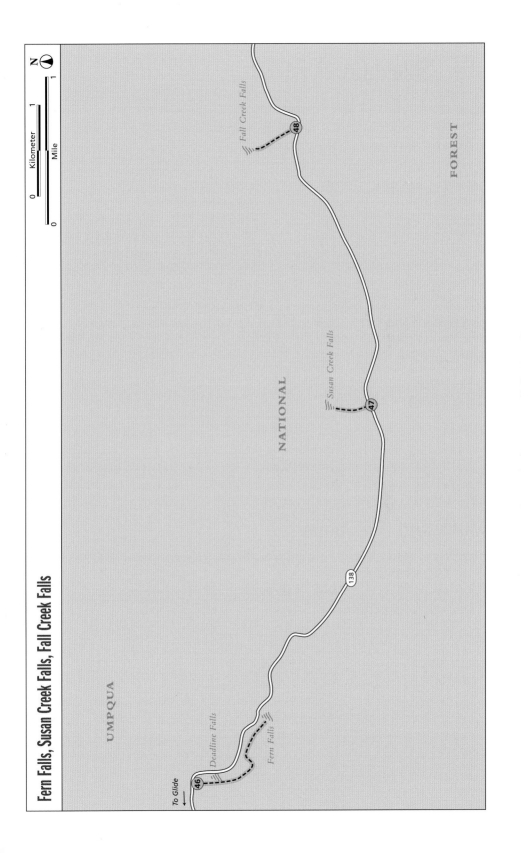

47 Susan Creek Falls

Because of the minimal distance and elevation gain, the short trek to Susan Creek Falls is perfect for families. The very explorable, swimmable, and picnic-ready area around the falls doesn't hurt things either.

See map on page 165.
Height: 50 feet
Distance: 1.4 miles out and back
Elevation gain: 170 feet
Difficulty: Easy
Trail surface: Hard-packed gravel, rocky
Hiking time: About 1 hour
County: Douglas

Land status: County park
Fees and permits: None
Trail contact: BLM in Roseburg, (541) 440-4930; http://www.blm.gov/or/districts/roseburg/index.php
Map: *DeLorme Atlas & Gazetteer Oregon,* page 54, B3

Finding the trailhead: From Roseburg, take exit 124 and drive east along OR 138 for 28 miles. Just past milepost 28 the parking area and trailhead to the falls is on the left. GPS: N43 17.938' / W122 54.363'

The Hike

The well-graded trail to Susan Creek Falls passes through a nice chunk of old-growth forest for a scant 0.7 mile before delivering you to the falls. As mentioned in the intro, if the family is along for the journey or if members of your party have hiking limitations, this one is ideal. The shaded grotto around Susan Creek Falls is complete with picnic benches, swimmable creek areas, and a beautiful, punchbowl-style falls.

Miles and Directions

0.0 From the trailhead, hike 0.7 mile to a viewing area and a footbridge leading across Susan Creek near the base of the falls.

0.7 Arrive at the falls (N43 18.296' / W122 54.440'). Head back the way you came.

1.4 Arrive back at the trailhead.

Susan Creek Falls

48 Fall Creek Falls

If you're a waterfall hunter on a time crunch, it can be difficult to pick and choose your way through the countless waterfalls in the Umpqua River area. Don't skip this one. The trip to Fall Creek Falls can satisfy several cravings often possessed by hikers. There's remarkable geology, eye-widening scenery, and, of course, a waterfall—a four-tiered, 120-foot waterfall at that.

See map on page 165.
Height: Main drop, 50 feet; 4 combined drops, 120 feet
Distance: 1.8 miles out and back
Elevation gain: 370 feet
Difficulty: Easy
Trail surface: Hard-packed dirt, rocky
Hiking time: About 1-2 hours
County: Douglas

Land status: National forest
Fees and permits: None
Trail contact: North Umpqua Ranger District, (541) 496-3532, http://www .fs.usda.gov/recarea/umpqua/null/ recarea/?recid=63384&actid=29
Map: *DeLorme Atlas & Gazetteer Oregon,* page 54, B3

Finding the trailhead: From Roseburg, take exit 124 and drive east along OR 138 for 32 miles. After milepost 32 look for the parking area and trailhead on the left. GPS: N43 18.800' / W122 50.119'

The Hike

This trail to Fall Creek Falls takes hikers through some fascinating volcanic geology. And it doesn't take long to do so. The hike starts by crossing a footbridge and shortly thereafter leads through a narrow bedrock crevice. Continue along the trail for 0.3 mile to a junction with the Job's Garden Trail. Stay straight here, hiking along the main trail.

Hike another 0.3 mile to the base of the falls. Along the way keep an eye out for stacks of columnar basalt. Occasionally these massive, honeycomb-shaped pillars jut out catawampus in all directions like a pile of twigs. The path also parallels the creek as it travels through narrow gorges and expands into broad, cedar-lined beaches.

This cascade has a vastly different appearance depending on the season, as do many of the falls in this area. Fall Creek Falls goes from thundering in spring to a delicate single spout from a basalt notch in summer. From the falls the trail switchbacks up another 0.3 mile to a gravel road, visiting the upper three tiers of the falls along the way. Head back the way you came to complete the hike.

Miles and Directions

0.0 From the trailhead, hike 0.3 mile to a junction with the Job's Garden Trail.

0.3 Arrive at a junction and continue straight for another 0.3 mile to the base of Fall Creek Falls (N43 19.118' / W122 50.369').

Fall Creek Falls

0.6 Continue up the trail as it switchbacks another 0.3 mile to a gravel road at the top of the falls.

0.9 Arrive at a gravel road. Head back the way you came.

1.8 Arrive back at the trailhead.

The trail to Fall Creek Falls

49 Shadow Falls

What you can see of it is beautiful. Shadow Falls twists and crashes through narrow rock cracks in three visible tiers.

Height: 75 feet over 3 combined drops
Distance: 1.6 miles out and back
Elevation gain: 320 feet
Difficulty: Easy
Trail surface: Hard-packed dirt, rocky
Hiking time: About 1 hour
County: Douglas
Land status: National forest

Fees and permits: None
Trail contact: Umpqua Ranger District, (541) 496-3532, http://www .fs.usda.gov/recarea/umpqua/null/ recarea/?recid=63384&actid=29
Map: *DeLorme Atlas & Gazetteer Oregon,* page 54, D2

Finding the trailhead: From the town of Glide, head south on Little River Road for 6.7 miles. Turn right at the covered bridge onto Cavitt Creek Road and drive for 12 miles, staying straight at all junctions to the signed trailhead on the right. GPS: N43 09.332' / W122 56.669'. Along the way Cavitt Creek Road becomes a very drivable gravel road and turns into OR 82 and then FR 25.

The Hike

After miles of gravel-road driving, you'll be happy to see the trailhead. And the hike to Shadow Falls is pretty straightforward. From the parking area, follow the path as it descends into the forest for 0.3 mile before arriving at a footbridge. The sometimes-brushy trail continues its descent through remarkable stands of old growth for another 0.4 mile before reaching a switchback and dropping the last 0.1 mile to the falls viewing area.

The viewing area is fenced off for a reason. Exercise caution here. The falls themselves are slightly elusive. Cavitt Creek weaves through cracks and shadows before

Shadow Falls

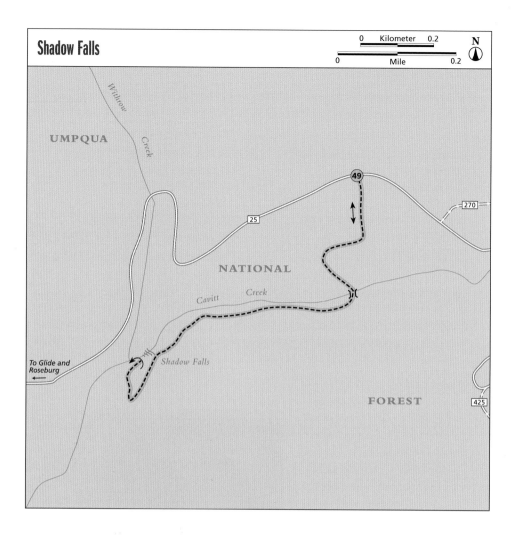

reemerging and tumbling its final 30 feet. Head back the way you came to return to the trailhead.

Miles and Directions

0.0   From the trailhead, hike 0.3 mile to a footbridge.

0.3   Arrive at a footbridge. Continue 0.5 mile.

0.8   Arrive at the fenced Shadow Falls viewing area. Head back the way you came.

1.6   Arrive back at the trailhead.

50 Wolf Creek Falls

The path that leads to Wolf Creek Falls is as good as old-growth hiking trails get. The casual stroll looks like a forest wonderland movie set, complete with serene creek pools, massive stands of timber, and as lush an understory as you'll find on any hike in this book. The upper and lower falls form the perfect crescendo for this walk through the woods.

Height: Upper Falls, 75 feet; Lower Falls, 20 feet

Distance: 2.4 miles out and back

Elevation gain: 370 feet

Difficulty: Easy

Trail surface: Hard-packed dirt, rocky

Hiking time: About 1-2 hours

County: Douglas

Land status: County park

Fees and permits: None

Trail contact: BLM in Roseburg, (541) 440-4930, http://www.blm.gov/or/districts/roseburg/index.php

Map: *DeLorme Atlas & Gazetteer Oregon,* page 54, C2

Finding the trailhead: From the town of Glide, head south onto Little River Road and drive 10.8 miles to the parking area and trailhead for Wolf Creek Falls on the right. GPS: N43 14.025' / W122 57.074'. If this area is full, there is overflow parking on the left side of the road.

Wolf Creek

The trail to Wolf Creek Falls

The Hike

From the trailhead, cross a 150-foot-long bridge over the Little River. Over the next 1.2 miles, the trail parallels the wildly scenic Wolf Creek before arriving at the lower falls. On a journey that gets better with every step, look for numerous spots to access

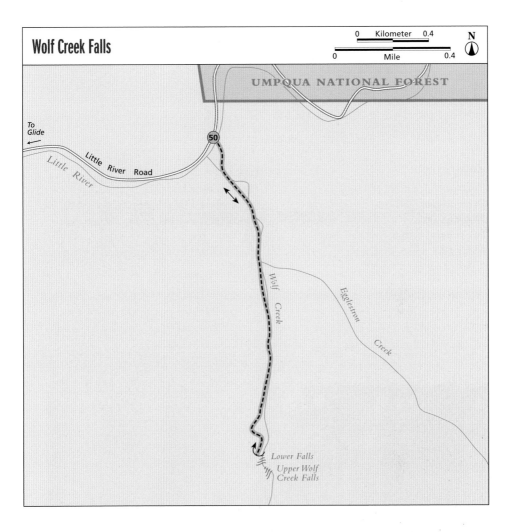

Wolf Creek Falls

Wolf Creek's bedrock pools and mini-falls and enjoy endless red huckleberries in summer.

Once at the lower falls, the trail continues a short way up to the viewing area for Upper Wolf Creek Falls. Enjoy the view and the huckleberries, then head back the way you came.

Miles and Directions

0.0 From the trailhead, cross the footbridge and hike 1.2 miles to Upper Wolf Creek Falls (N43 13.116' / W122 56.909'), passing the lower falls (N43 13.148' / W122 56.910') just prior.

1.2 Arrive at Upper Wolf Creek Falls. Head back the way you came.

2.4 Arrive back at the trailhead.

51 Grotto Falls

Super-short, super-sweet. After a couple of switchbacks through second-growth forest, you are delivered to a lush, old-growth canyon and the twin cascades of Grotto Falls. The path leads to a cave behind the falls, which you can reach out and safely touch during low-water season.

Height: 80 feet
Distance: 0.6 mile out and back
Elevation gain: 180 feet
Difficulty: Easy
Trail surface: Hard-packed dirt, rocky
Hiking time: About 30 minutes
County: Douglas

Land status: National forest
Fees and permits: None
Trail contact: BLM in Roseburg, (541) 440-4930, http://www.blm.gov/or/districts/roseburg/index.php
Map: *DeLorme Atlas & Gazetteer Oregon,* page 54, C3

Finding the trailhead: From the town of Glide, head south onto Little River Road and drive 16 miles. Turn left onto gravel FR 2703, across from the Cool Water Campground, and drive 4.4 miles to a junction with FR 2703-150. Follow this road and signs for Grotto Falls for another 2 miles to the trailhead immediately after a bridge. GPS: N43 14.902' / W122 49.411'

Behind Grotto Falls

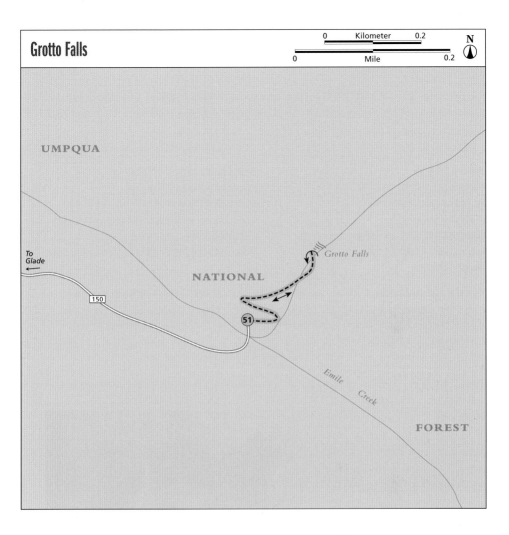

The Hike

From the trailhead, the path climbs a handful of switchbacks, rounds a corner, and delivers you to Grotto Falls. There's plenty of room to explore behind the falls—a great place for a snack or lunch.

Miles and Directions

0.0   From the trailhead, hike 0.3 mile to Grotto Falls.

0.3   Arrive at Grotto Falls (N43 14.996' / W122 49.308'). Head back the way you came.

0.6   Arrive back at the trailhead.

52 Yakso Falls

An easy, well-graded trail leads to the bottom of a deep canyon and Yakso Falls. In low-water conditions it's possible to walk along tree roots to an exquisite rock beach perfect for a picnic and rock skipping.

Height: 50 feet
Distance: 1.4 miles out and back
Elevation gain: 260 feet
Difficulty: Easy
Trail surface: Hard-packed dirt, rocky
Hiking time: About 1 hour
County: Douglas

Land status: National forest
Fees and permits: None
Trail contact: BLM in Roseburg, (541) 440-4930, http://www.blm.gov/or/districts/roseburg/index.php
Map: *DeLorme Atlas & Gazetteer Oregon,* page 54, C4

Finding the trailhead: From the town of Glide, head south onto Little River Road and drive 25.8 miles, the last seven being easy gravel, to Lake in the Woods Campground. Trailhead parking is at the campground entrance. The Yakso Falls Trail is across the road from the campground entrance. GPS: N43 13.085' / W122 43.438'

The Hike

From the roadside trailhead, hike 0.3 mile to a very low, potentially no-flow creek crossing where a footbridge used to be. The trail continues a mild ascent before rounding a corner and descending to the bottom of a canyon and the base of Yakso Falls after 0.7 mile of total hiking.

The beach area near the base of the falls will only be accessible during the low-flow months of summer. And even then you have to climb along some tree roots and potentially get your feet wet to access the rocky beach. It's worth bringing the water shoes, however, as the delicate falls and

Yakso Falls

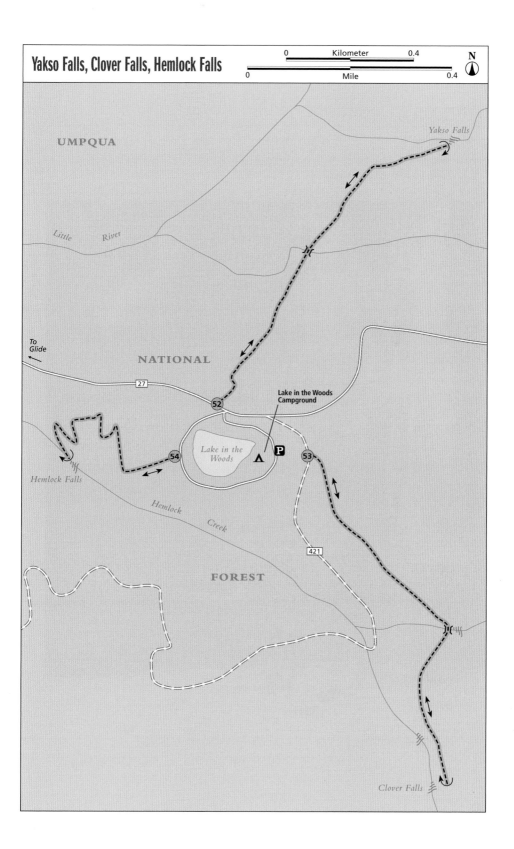

Yakso Falls, Clover Falls, Hemlock Falls

0   Kilometer   0.4

0   Mile   0.4

N

UMPQUA

Yakso Falls

Little   River

To
Glide

NATIONAL

27

52

Lake in the Woods
Campground

Lake in the
Woods

P

Λ

54

53

Hemlock Falls

Hemlock

Creek

421

FOREST

Clover Falls

flourishing canyon both require thorough inspection. Then head back the way you came.

Miles and Directions

0.0 From the trailhead, hike 0.7 mile to the base of Yakso Falls.

0.7 Arrive at Yakso Falls (N43 13.474' / W122 42.947'). Head back the way you came.

1.4 Arrive back at the trailhead.

Rock skipping at Yakso Falls

53 Clover Falls

The hike to Clover Falls starts in unremarkable second-growth forest that soon transforms into dramatic old growth. Numerous falls can be seen along the way including a gorgeous dual cascade beneath a footbridge. Be forewarned, however: To get a decent look at Clover Falls itself, you must endeavor a steep scramble to the base.

See map on page 179.
Height: 40 feet
Distance: 2.2 miles out and back
Elevation gain: 560 feet
Difficulty: Easy to moderate
Trail surface: Hard-packed dirt, rocky, loose rock
Hiking time: About 1-2 hours

County: Douglas
Land status: National forest
Fees and permits: None
Trail contact: BLM in Roseburg, (541) 440-4930, http://www.blm.gov/or/districts/roseburg/index.php
Map: *DeLorme Atlas & Gazetteer Oregon,* page 54, C4

Finding the trailhead: From the town of Glide, head south onto Little River Road and drive 25.8 miles, the last seven being easy gravel, to the Lake in the Woods Campground. A couple hundred feet past the campground, turn right onto FR 421. Drive a couple hundred more feet and arrive at the signed trail leading to Clover Falls on the left. GPS: N43 13.004' / W122 43.250'

The Hike

The hike begins with a steady ascent through relatively new forest for 0.5 mile before arriving at a footbridge. Just before the bridge you can catch a glimpse of some falls, but continue over the bridge. The view of the twin-cascade that passes beneath the bridge is better from the other side.

Once over the bridge the forest changes dramatically. The path now climbs steadily through groves of stately old growth. Continue another 0.6 mile, passing a couple of small cascades along the way, to an obscured view of Clover Falls. For a better view, backtrack slightly and find a path that's suitable down to the creek. Head back the way you came.

Miles and Directions

0.0 From the trailhead, hike 0.5 mile to a footbridge.

0.5 Arrive at a footbridge. Continue hiking for another 0.6 mile.

1.1 Arrive at an obstructed view of Clover Falls (N43 12.391' / W122 42.945'). Head back the way you came.

2.2 Arrive back at the trailhead.

54 Hemlock Falls

Perhaps the most photogenic of the falls near the Lake in the Woods Campground, Hemlock Falls is accessed via an easy, steady descent to an approachable falls area.

See map on page 179.
Height: 45 feet
Distance: 1.0 mile out and back
Elevation gain: 300 feet
Difficulty: Easy
Trail surface: Hard-packed dirt, rocky
Hiking time: About 30 minutes to 1 hour
County: Douglas

Land status: National forest
Fees and permits: None
Trail contact: BLM in Roseburg, (541) 440-4930, http://www.blm.gov/or/districts/roseburg/index.php
Map: *DeLorme Atlas & Gazetteer Oregon*, page 54, C4

Finding the trailhead: From the town of Glide, head south onto Little River Road and drive 25.8 miles, the last seven being easy gravel, to Lake in the Woods Campground. Pull into the campground and park at the day-use area on the right. Continue walking along the main campground road a couple hundred feet to a marked hiking trail near campsite #1. GPS: N43 12.998' / W122 43.546'

The Hike

The trail to Hemlock Falls is a steady, somewhat steep descent with a couple of switchbacks thrown in to break up the monotony. After 0.5 mile of hiking, the trail drops you off at the base of Hemlock Falls. The area surrounding the falls is very green, very lush. It is also easy to maneuver around the area to gain numerous vantages of the cascade as it dips and drops from a narrow chasm into a shallow splash pool.

Miles and Directions

0.0 From the trailhead, descend 0.5 mile to the falls.
0.5 Arrive at Hemlock Falls (N43 12.998' / W122 43.758'). Head back the way you came.
1.0 Arrive back at the trailhead.

Hemlock Falls

55 Columnar/Surprise Falls

While both falls are springs, they are quite different. And Columnar Falls ranks near the top of the list in terms of notable cascades in the state of Oregon. Bear in mind that the trail leading to these falls starts at the Umpqua Hot Springs. Between the hot springs and the cold springs, you can expect a rather eclectic group. If you plan on visiting the hot springs while you're there, remember that nudity is common.

Height: 25 feet
Distance: 0.5 mile out and back
Elevation: 150 feet
Difficulty: Easy
Trail surface: Hard-packed dirt, rocky
Hiking time: About 30 minutes
County: Douglas
Land status: National forest

Fees and permits: Northwest Forest Pass or small day-use fee required
Trail contact: Diamond Lake Ranger District, (541) 498-2531, http://www .fs.usda.gov/recarea/umpqua/null/ recarea/?recid=63378&actid=31
Map: *DeLorme Atlas & Gazetteer Oregon,* page 55, B8

Finding the trailhead: From the town of Glide, head east on OR 138 for 42.5 miles. At milepost 59 turn left onto Toketee-Rigdon Road. After 0.2 mile stay left and continue 2 miles. Take a right onto FR 3401 and drive just over 2 more miles to the parking area for the Umpqua Hot Springs on the left. GPS: N43 17.602' / W122 21.902'

Columnar Falls

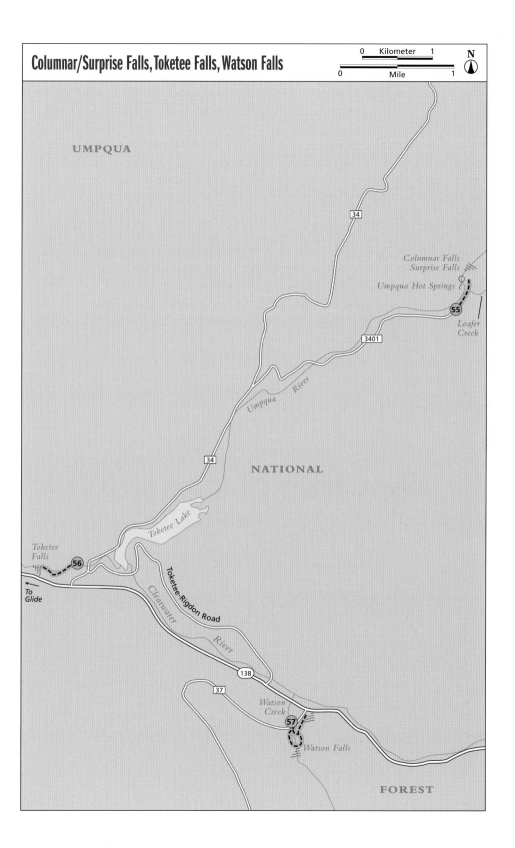

Columnar/Surprise Falls, Toketee Falls, Watson Falls

UMPQUA

34

Columnar Falls
Surprise Falls

Umpqua Hot Springs

55

Loafer
Creek

3401

Umpqua   River

34

NATIONAL

Toketee Lake

Toketee
Falls

56

To
Glide

Toketee-Rigdon Road

Clearwater

River

138

37

Watson
Creek

57

Watson Falls

FOREST

The Hike

Begin by walking back to the gravel road and continue up the left shoulder for a hundred feet or so to an unmarked path that leads down into the woods. The trail crosses a creek and after 0.25 mile passes over the top of Surprise Falls—a spring that launches out of the hillside just under the trail. Just beyond Surprise Falls the path descends down to Columnar Falls. The ethereal cascade composed of a spring emerges at the top of a wall of columnar basalt. It then cascades down its face before almost magically vanishing back into the ground.

Miles and Directions

0.0 From the parking area, walk back to the gravel road and continue up the left shoulder for a hundred feet or so and take the unmarked path that leads down into the woods.

0.1 Continue hiking for 0.2 mile to Surprise and Columnar Falls.

0.25 Arrive at Surprise Falls (N43 17.785' / W122 21.758') then Columnar Falls (N43 17.812' / W122 21.772'). Head back the way you came.

0.5 Arrive back at the parking area.

56 Toketee Falls

The main draw along the OR 138 corridor, Toketee Falls is a favorite among photographers and casual travelers alike. Framed by visually stunning columnar basalt, it stands to reason that the name Toketee means "pretty" in Northwest Chinook jargon.

See map on page 185.
Height: Main drop, 85 feet; upper drop, 28 feet
Distance: 0.8 mile out and back
Elevation gain: 165 feet
Difficulty: Easy
Trail surface: Hard-packed dirt, rocky, stairs, catwalks

Hiking time: About 30 minutes
County: Douglas
Land status: National forest
Fees and permits: None
Trail contact: Diamond Lake Ranger District, (541) 498-2531
Map: *DeLorme Atlas & Gazetteer Oregon,* page 55, C7

Finding the trailhead: From the town of Glide, head east on OR 138 for 42.5 miles. At milepost 59 turn left onto Toketee-Rigdon Road. Drive 0.4 mile, following signs to the Toketee Falls parking area. GPS: N43 15.842' / W122 25.646'

The Hike

From the trailhead, follow the trail for 0.4 mile as it parallels the North Umqua River. The trail occasionally morphs into well-railed staircases that cling to panoramic canyon walls before arriving at a wooden viewing platform. The elevated view affords the classic, though frustratingly distant, view of Toketee Falls. Hike back the way you came.

Miles and Directions

0.0 From the trailhead, hike 0.4 mile to the viewing platform.
0.4 Arrive at the viewing platform for Toketee Falls (N43 15.823' / W122 26.005'). Head back the way you came.
0.8 Arrive back at the trailhead.

Toketee Falls

Watson Falls

57 Watson Falls

The tallest waterfall in southwest Oregon and billed as the third tallest in the state, Watson Falls is the most impressive falls in the area. The quick loop hike that visits the falls presents visitors with a pleasant view early on. But you owe it to yourself to take the side trail that climbs to a more intimate and memorable view.

See map on page 185.
Height: 293 feet
Distance: 1.0-mile loop
Elevation gain: 340 feet
Difficulty: Easy
Trail surface: Hard-packed dirt, rocky
Hiking time: About 30 minutes
County: Douglas

Land status: National forest
Fees and permits: None
Trail contact: Diamond Lake Ranger District, (541) 498-2531, http://www .fs.usda.gov/recarea/umpqua/null/ recarea/?recid=63378&actid=31
Map: *DeLorme Atlas & Gazetteer Oregon,* page 55, C8

Finding the trailhead: From the town of Glide, head east on OR 138 for 45 miles. After mile marker 62 turn right onto Fish Creek Road and proceed another 0.2 mile to the parking area on the right. GPS: N43 14.730' / W122 23.495'

The Hike

From the trailhead near the parking area turnaround, follow the main path up to a road crossing. The trail picks up on the other side of the road and begins a steady 0.3 mile climb to a footbridge across Watson Creek.

The trail soon passes by a tranquil creek-side viewing area and arrives at a junction. Follow the ascending path to the left for 0.1 mile to a viewing area of Watson Falls. Backtrack to the junction and head left to complete the loop. When the trail reaches the road again, cross and make a right. Walk along the shoulder of the road a short way to pick up the trail leading down to the left and back to the parking area.

Miles and Directions

0.0 From the trailhead, hike a few hundred feet, cross a road, and continue 0.3 mile to a junction.

0.3 Arrive at a junction. Take a left and hike 0.1 mile to a viewing area for Watson Falls (N43 14.785' / W122 23.383').

0.5 Arrive at Watson Falls. Backtrack to the trail junction.

0.6 Arrive at trail junction. Make a left and hike 0.4 mile back to the trailhead.

1.0 Arrive back at the trailhead.

58 Warm Springs Falls

Often completely overlooked by those heading to Lemolo Falls, the trek to Warm Springs Falls is brief, but the falls exhibit some classic columnar basalt beauty that is the hallmark of a number of more popular Northwest hikes.

Height: 60 feet
Distance: 0.6 mile out and back
Elevation gain: 40 feet
Difficulty: Easy
Trail surface: Hard-packed dirt, duffy
Hiking time: About 30 minutes
County: Douglas County
Land status: National forest

Fees and permits: None
Trail contact: Diamond Lake Ranger District, (541) 498-2531, http://www.fs.usda.gov/recarea/umpqua/null/recarea/?recid=63378&actid=31
Map: *DeLorme Atlas & Gazetteer Oregon,* page 55, A9–B9

Finding the trailhead: From the town of Glide, head east on OR 138 for 56.4 miles. Turn left onto FR 2610 and drive 5 miles. Cross the Lemolo Lake Dam and stay left. Drive for 3 miles and turn left onto FR 680. Continue 1.6 miles to a small pullout on the left for the Warm Springs Falls Trail. GPS: N43 21.483' / W122 14.426'

The Hike

From the trailhead the path leads gently through a pleasant forest for just 0.3 mile, arriving at a viewpoint of Warm Springs Falls. Admirably framed by rhododendrons in spring, the 60-foot curtain–style falls have a strong flow even in summer. Enjoy the view and head back the way you came.

Miles and Directions

0.0 From the trailhead, hike 0.3 mile to the falls viewpoint.

0.3 Arrive at the Warm Springs Falls viewpoint (N43 21.448' / W122 14.713'). Head back the way you came.

0.6 Arrive at the trailhead.

Warm Springs Falls

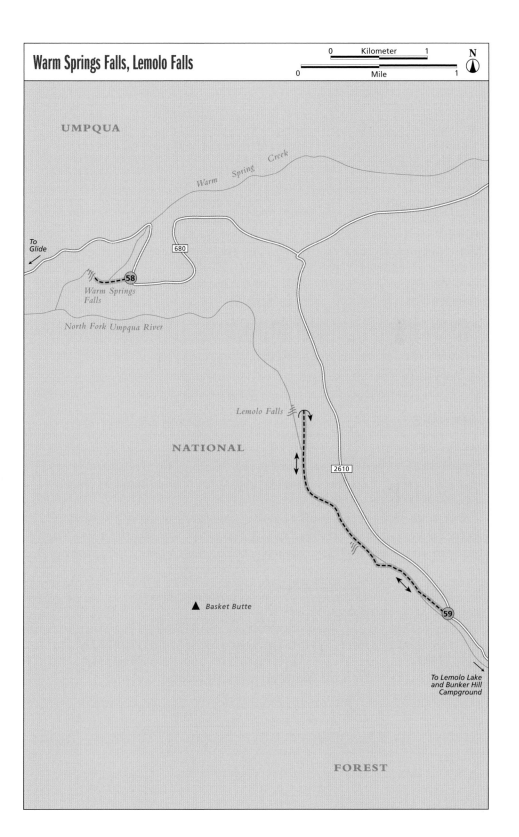

Warm Springs Falls, Lemolo Falls

UMPQUA

Warm Spring Creek

To Glide

680

58

Warm Springs Falls

North Fork Umpqua River

NATIONAL

Lemolo Falls

2610

▲ Basket Butte

59

To Lemolo Lake and Bunker Hill Campground

FOREST

0 Kilometer 1

0 Mile 1

N

59 Lemolo Falls

The tallest falls on the North Umpqua River, Lemolo is also one of the most consistent in terms of flow—thanks in large part to the dam just up river. However, the mini-cascades and pools that occupy the river from the trailhead to the falls are arguably the best part of the hike.

See map on page 191.
Height: 165 feet
Distance: 3.4 miles out and back
Elevation gain: 520 feet
Difficulty: Easy to moderate
Trail surface: Hard-packed dirt, rocky
Hiking time: About 1.5-3 hours

County: Douglas County
Land status: National forest
Fees and permits: None
Trail contact: Diamond Lake Ranger District, (541) 498-2531
Map: *DeLorme Atlas & Gazetteer Oregon,* page 55, B9

Finding the trailhead: From the town of Glide, head east on OR 138 for 56.4 miles. Turn left onto FR 2610 and drive 5 miles. Cross the Lemolo Lake Dam and stay left. Drive for 0.6 mile and cross a bridge on the left that crosses a canal and arrives at a parking area for Lemolo Falls. GPS: N43 19.748' / W122 12.166'

The Hike

From the parking area the trail starts out with a long, steady descent to the North Umpqua River. Small rivulets occasionally cross the trail as the river itself becomes increasingly alluring. Look for boot paths leading to some of the more desirable swimming holes and picnic spots.

After 1.7 miles of hiking, you'll encounter a side view of the falls. If this view isn't quite good enough, backtrack about 0.3 mile and look for a somewhat easy river crossing over a downed tree. After a short climb of a couple hundred feet up the riverbank, you'll encounter a trail. Turn right here and hike for 1 mile, staying right at a junction, until the path ends near the base of the falls.

Miles and Directions

0.0 From the trailhead, hike 1.7 miles to a partial view of Lemolo Falls (N43 20.777' / W122 13.188').

1.7 Arrive at a viewpoint of Lemolo Falls. Head back the way you came.

3.4 Arrive back at the trailhead.

60 Rough Rider Falls

The hike to Rough Rider Falls affords the chance to visit the Rouge River in its infancy. Just a handful of miles from the headwaters of the spring-born river, the falls are forceful and the river is gorgeous. It's trails like this that make hiking in southern Oregon a joy. Beauty and solitude in large, equal doses are not uncommon in this part of the state. Similar trails would draw throngs elsewhere. But just a stone's throw away from Crater Lake, Rough Rider Falls sits strong and proud, in relative obscurity. Teddy Roosevelt, the Father of Conservation, would be proud.

Height: 30 feet
Distance: 6.5 miles out and back
Elevation gain: 870 feet
Difficulty: Moderate
Trail surface: Hard-packed dirt, duffy
Hiking time: About 3-4 hours
County: Douglas County
Land status: National forest

Fees and permits: None
Trail contact: High Cascades Ranger District, (541) 560-3400, http://www.fs.usda.gov/recarea/rogue-siskiyou/null/recarea/?recid=69452&actid=33
Map: DeLorme Atlas & Gazetteer Oregon, page 55, E8

Finding the trailhead: From Medford, take OR 62 east for 57 miles. Stay straight on OR 230 toward Diamond Lake for another 12 miles. Just after milepost 12, make a right onto FR 6530 at a sign for Hamaker Campground. Drive 0.6 mile and stay left at a fork to remain on 6530. Drive another 0.2 mile to a very small pullout on the right, directly across from a trail on the left side of the road. GPS: N43 03.922' W122 19.448'

The Hike

From the pullout, cross the gravel road and, ignoring a trail to the left, follow the path leading to the right and into the woods. Save for one brief encounter, the trail avoids the Rogue River for the first 1.5 miles of the hike before finally descending down to it. Soon after, the trail passes by a twisting, churning cascade that requires a short scramble for a better view.

The trail now begins a long, steady ascent. But the quality of the scenery here escalates in kind. After another mile-plus of hiking, a walk across a downed tree is required to stay out of a small marsh. Just 0.4 mile later, before a switchback, look for a boot path leading down near the base of the audible Rough Rider Falls. There are a few nice spots for a picnic along the banks of the river, but the best vantage is from a small island in the middle of the turbulent water. Depending on conditions, the island can be reached via rock hop or a downed tree. The water here is fast and powerful, however, so exercise extreme caution. The falls aren't all that large in terms of height, but they are powerful. The clean, turbulent waters of the Rogue make the area around the falls a place you can spend a whole lot of quality time. Then head back the way you came.

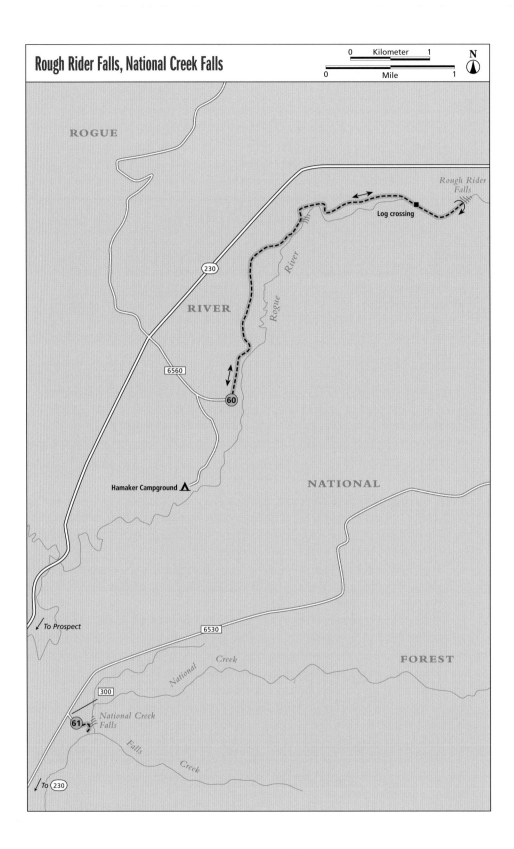

Rough Rider Falls, National Creek Falls

Rogue River
Rough Rider Falls
Log crossing
230
RIVER
Rogue River
6560
60
Hamaker Campground
NATIONAL
To Prospect
6530
FOREST
Creek
National Creek
300
61
National Creek Falls
Falls
Creek
To 230

Miles and Directions

0.0 From the trailhead, hike 1.7 miles.

1.7 Arrive at an unnamed falls (N43 05.049' / W122 18.809'). Continue hiking.

3.25 Arrive at a switchback and the boot path (N43 05.139' / W122 17.458') leading to the river near the base of Rough Rider Falls (N43 05.147' / W122 17.430'). Head back the way you came.

6.5 Arrive back at the trailhead.

Rough Rider Falls

61 National Creek Falls

Spring-fed cascades are a sure thing for waterfall lovers. Low snowpack, dry winter, long summer—no problem. The sun rises, and spring-fed falls are full. National Creek Falls near Crater Lake National Park is one such dandy. At just under a mile, it might barely qualify as a hike, but it is thoroughly impressive and very photogenic.

See map on page 194.
Height: 40 feet
Distance: 0.8 mile out and back
Elevation gain: 170 feet
Difficulty: Easy
Trail surface: Hard-packed dirt
Hiking time: About 30 minutes to 1 hour
County: Douglas County

Land status: National forest
Fees and permits: None
Trail contact: High Cascades Ranger District, (541) 560-3400, http://www.fs .usda.gov/recarea/rogue-siskiyou/null/ recarea/?recid=69452&actid=33
Map: *DeLorme Atlas & Gazetteer Oregon,* page 55, E8

Finding the trailhead: From the Historic Prospect Hotel in Prospect, Oregon, head north on OR 62 for 12 miles to a junction with OR 230. Continue straight on OR 230 for 6 more miles to FR 6530. Make a right onto FR 6530 and drive 1.3 miles. Stay left at a fork to remain on FR 6530, continue 2.4 miles, and turn right onto FR 300. Follow this bumpy gravel road for less than 0.25 mile to the road's end at the National Falls parking area. GPS: N43 01.895' / W122 20.818'

The Hike

From the parking area, follow the wide dirt path trail as it switchbacks steadily for 0.4 mile to the base of National Creek Falls. Along the way the trail comes into close contact with the top of the falls and a number of dicey boot paths leading to precarious viewpoints. It's best to stay the course here, especially if kids are in tow, and make your way to the much better views and explore the area at the bottom of the falls.

Miles and Directions

0.0 From the trailhead, hike 0.4 mile to the base of the falls.
0.4 Hike back the way you came.
0.8 Arrive back at the trailhead.

National Creek Falls

62 Plaikni Falls

The trail to Plaikni Falls opened in the summer of 2011. It's hard to imagine that there was something else hiding at Crater Lake National Park all this time, but here it is, Plaikni Falls. It's not a tall cascade—with the main drop only being an estimated 20 feet. But the water continues a steep and turbulent descent along a creek lined with wildflowers. While it might not be in the same league as the little lake over the ridge, it's certainly worth dedicating an hour toward, especially during the peak of late summer wildflowers.

Height: 20 feet
Distance: 2.0 miles out and back
Elevation gain: 200 feet
Difficulty: Easy
Trail surface: Compacted gravel, hard-packed dirt
Hiking time: About 1 hour

County: Klammath
Land status: National park
Fees and permits: National park fees apply
Trail contact: National Park Service, (541) 594-3000, www.nps.gov/crla/index.htm
Map: *DeLorme Atlas & Gazetteer Oregon,* page 63, A6

Finding the trailhead: From Rim Village, drive south 2.8 miles toward OR 62. Make a left onto East Rim Drive and go 8.5 miles. Make a right on Pinnacles Road and drive 1.2 miles to the pullout and trailhead on the left. GPS: N42 54.113' / W122 03.643'

The Hike

The trail to Plaikni Falls starts out through a level, somewhat sparsely populated forest of old-growth hemlock and fir. The trail is wide and complemented by a number of benches along the winding route. After a pleasant warm-up through the woods, the trail skirts by the scenic Anderson Bluffs and then meets up with Sand Creek.

The trail then takes on a much different feel as it begins a steady but well-graded ascent alongside the spring-fed creek before arriving at the falls-viewing area. In summer, wildflowers eagerly crowd the creek on either side during the final stretch of the hike. The falls themselves are

Plaikni Falls

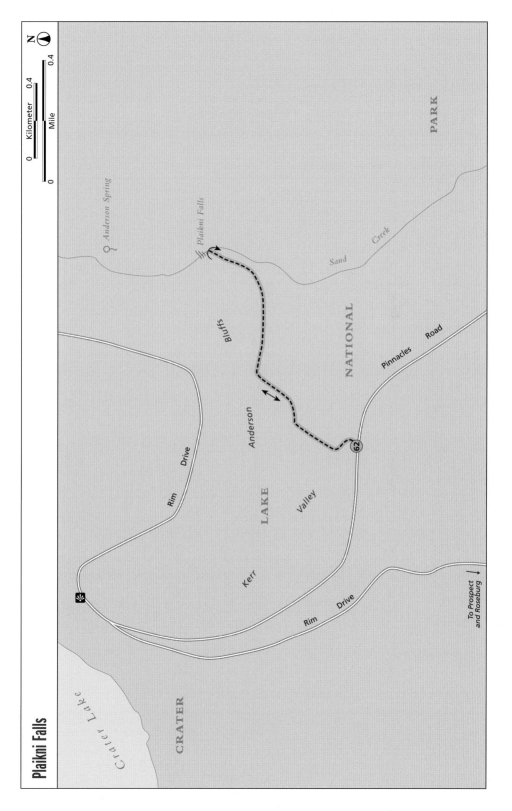

Plaikni Falls

N

also framed nicely with colorful flora, making for quite a photogenic turnaround point.

Miles and Directions

0.0 From the trailhead, hike along the gravel path for 0.5 mile.

0.5 Arrive at the Anderson Bluffs. Continue on the trail for another 0.5 mile to Plaikni Falls (N42 54.536' / W122 02.918').

1.0 Head back the way you came.

2.0 Arrive back at the trailhead.

63 Pearsoney Falls

Waterfalls don't have to be big. Of course, skyscraper-size, thundering cascades are awe-inspiring and majestic. But smaller falls can be beautiful, peaceful, and just as worthy of your time. Pearsoney Falls is a prime example of the latter. The falls itself was named after a pair of families that settled in the Prospect area, the Pearsons and the Mooneys.

Height: 12 feet
Distance: 0.5 mile out and back
Elevation gain: 100 feet
Difficulty: Easy
Trail surface: Hard-packed dirt
Hiking time: About 30 minutes
County: Jackson

Land status: State park
Fees and permits: None
Trail contact: Oregon Parks and Recreation Department, (541) 560-3334, oregonstate parks.org
Map: *DeLorme Atlas & Gazetteer Oregon,* page 62, C2

Finding the trailhead: From the Historic Prospect Hotel in Prospect, Oregon, drive south on Mill Creek Drive for 0.2 mile to the Pearsoney Falls parking area on the left. The trailhead is at the north end of the parking area. GPS: N42 44.885' / W122 29.499'

Pearsoney Falls

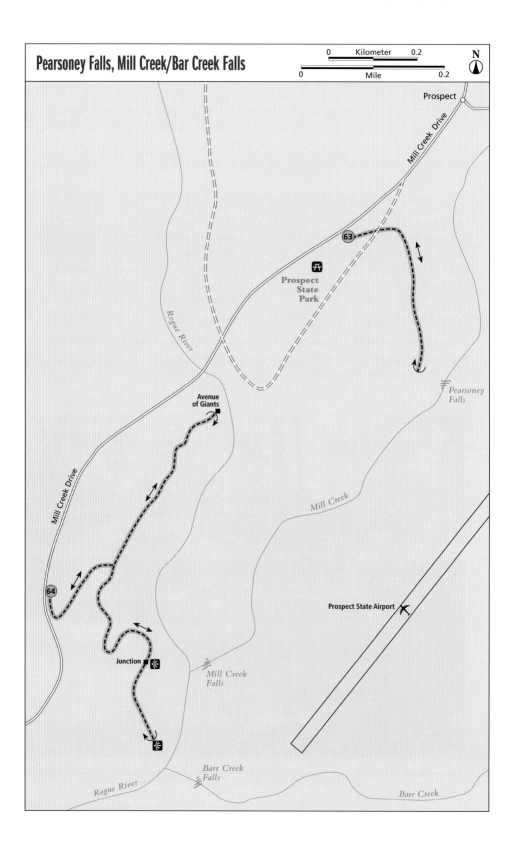

Pearsoney Falls, Mill Creek/Bar Creek Falls

0   Kilometer   0.2

0   Mile   0.2

N

Prospect

Mill Creek Drive

63

Prospect State Park

Pearsoney Falls

Rogue River

Mill Creek

Avenue of Giants

Mill Creek Drive

64

Prospect State Airport

Junction

Mill Creek Falls

Barr Creek Falls

Rogue River

Barr Creek

The Hike

You don't necessarily need to whip out your compass and map for this one, but we're not here to judge. From the trailhead, hike 180 feet or so to a gravel road crossing. The trail picks up immediately on the other side of the road and descends easily through pleasant woods for a total of 0.2 mile to Pearsoney Falls. The trail continues a short way down to the Rogue River.

Miles and Directions

0.0   From the trailhead, hike a couple hundred feet, cross a gravel road, and continue along the descending trail for 0.25 mile to Pearsoney Falls (GPS: N42 44.750' / W122 29.405').

0.2   Head back the way you came.

0.5   Arrive back at the trailhead.

64 Mill Creek/Barr Creek Falls

Two very large waterfalls and access to a scenic and geologically intriguing segment of the Rogue River highlight this 1.6-mile hike.

See map on page 202.

Height: Mill Creek Falls, 173 feet; Barr Creek Falls, 240 feet (combined drops)

Distance: 1.6 miles out and back

Elevation gain: 300 feet

Difficulty: Easy

Trail surface: Hard-packed dirt, rocks

Hiking time: About 30 minutes to 2 hours

County: Jackson

Land status: State park

Fees and permits: None

Trail contact: Oregon Parks and Recreation Department, (541) 560-3334, oregonstate parks.org

Map: *DeLorme Atlas & Gazetteer Oregon,* page 62, C2

Finding the trailhead: From the Historic Prospect Hotel in Prospect, Oregon, drive south on Mill Creek Drive for 0.9 mile. The parking area for the Prospect State Scenic Viewpoint, formerly the Mill Creek Falls Scenic area, is on the left. The trailhead is at the south end of the parking area. GPS: N42 44.493' / W122 29.979'

The Hike

Hiking in this area can be a little confusing. There are a number of spur trails and boot paths that closely resemble official trails. Just remember that any junctions of consequence are marked with a hitching post. Not all posts mark junctions, but all official junctions have posts. We'll get through this together.

From the trailhead, the path descends gently into the forest before hitting a switchback and then quickly encountering what looks like your first trail junction. Pay it no heed. Continue hiking 0.2 mile from the trailhead to a junction (hitching post). If you have the time and interest, stay to the left here and continue hiking for another 0.3 mile to a signed junction. To the left a quick path visits the Avenue of Giants—a set of passenger vehicle–size boulders and a nice view of the canyon. The path to the right descends down to the river in a series of interesting and occasionally sketchy routes down to the Rouge River. Once this area has been satisfactorily explored, backtrack up to the first official junction and veer left, continuing downriver.

Staying on the main trail, hike another 0.2 mile to another hitching post. To the left, a handful of spur trails lead to cross-canyon views of the massive Mill Creek Falls. From the hitching post junction, continue a short distance downriver to a set of steps and some precarious viewpoints of the multitiered Barr Creek Falls.

Miles and Directions

0.0 From the trailhead, hike 0.2 mile to the first official junction and stay left.

0.2 Continue 0.3 mile to a signed junction. To the left the trail leads 100 feet through a set

Barr Creek Falls

of boulders to the Avenue of Giants (N42 44.685' / W122 29.704'). To the right the trail descends to a series of paths down to the Rogue River. Explore at will and then backtrack to the first official junction.

0.6 Make a left and continue downriver for 0.2 mile to a large open area marked by a hitching post. A set of short trails to the left lead to views of Mill Creek Falls (N42 44.408' / W122 29.819'). Continue on the main trail a short way to viewpoints of Barr Creek Falls (N42 44.327' / W122 29.824').

1.0 Hike back the way you came, ascending for 0.6 mile back to the trailhead.

1.6 Arrive back at the trailhead.

Honorable Mentions

O. Steamboat Falls

These 20-foot falls are a popular swimming spot in summer and flow impressively in spring.

To visit the falls from the town of Glide, take OR 138 east for 22.5 miles and take a left onto Steamboat Creek Road. Drive 5.3 more miles to a turnout for the Steamboat Springs Campground. Drive another 0.5 mile to the campground and the falls (N43 22.420' / W122 38.441').

P. Whitehorse Falls

It's only 14 feet tall, but it's a beauty. And the pool and area below the falls are fantastic. The Whitehorse Falls Campground is located next to the day-use area.

Whitehorse Falls

To visit the falls from the town of Glide, travel east on OR 138 for 49.5 miles to the Whitehorse Falls Campground on the left. Park at the day-use area and walk a short distance to the falls (N43 14.867' / W122 18.300').

Q. Clearwater Falls

The 30-foot Clearwater Falls is very photogenic waterfall, though lighting can be tough. The creek below the falls is also a great picnic spot.

From the town of Glide, take OR 138 east for 54 miles to the Clearwater Falls Campground on the right. The falls are a short walk from the day-use parking area (N43 14.933' / W122 13.667').

R. Vidae Falls

Totaling 115 feet, Vidae Falls is located just off of Rim Drive in Crater Lake National Park. The falls play host to a number of brightly colored wildflowers in summer.

To visit the falls from Crater Lake Park Headquarters, take Rim Drive for 3 miles to the pullout at the base of Vidae Falls (N42 53.065' / W122 06.006').

Vidae Falls

S. Rogue River Gorge Falls

The Rogue River Gorge Falls is a delightful 30-foot cascade located at the Rogue Gorge viewpoint area. The Rogue is pinched into a slot canyon 10 feet wide just below the falls. Just up the road, the Natural Bridges Campground is home to a lava tube that swallows a good portion of the river and then spits it out a couple hundred feet away. Both are incredibly fascinating visits with informative interpretive signs along the way.

To visit the Rogue River Gorge Falls, drive 11.5 miles north (or east) from the town of Prospect on OR 62 to a signed parking area on the left. Follow the paved path down to the river. To visit the natural bridges, backtrack down OR 62 for less than a mile to the Natural Bridges Campground and follow signs to the day-use area. Walk the short path down to the natural bridges.

About the Author

Adam Sawyer is a writer, photographer, and tour guide based out of Portland, Oregon. As a freelance writer and photographer, his work has appeared in *Northwest Travel Magazine, Portland Monthly,* and *Columbia River Gorge* magazine. He pens articles as the Portland Hiking Examiner for examiner.com and authored the biweekly column Portland Family Outdoors for Craigmore Creations. He also co-hosted the KEEN HybridLife Radio Show for its duration and now serves as an ambassador for the company.